The Warrior Pharaohs

Over one 2,000-year period Egypt produced several fighting generals who belied the general impression of modern times that early Egyptians were not a warlike people. During that 2,000 years the Egyptians rose to throw off foreign invaders or themselves invaded neighboring kingdoms. The stories of these fighting generals, the Warrior Pharaohs, and the people they inspired to serve as valiant soldiers are told by an eminent student of Ancient Egypt, Leonard Cottrell.

The Warrior Pharaohs

by
Leonard Cottrell

G. P. PUTNAM'S SONS, NEW YORK

To "Dee"
and to the memory of
Flight-Lieutenant Basil Demetrios Bonakis, R.A.F.,
killed in action
7 January 1945

First American Edition 1969
Copyright © 1969 by Leonard Cottrell

Library of Congress Catalog Card Number: 68-24509

MANUFACTURED IN THE UNITED STATES OF AMERICA
12216

Contents

Acknowledgments

The author and publishers are indebted to the following for permission to quote copyright material: Princeton University Press, Princeton, New Jersey; the University of Chicago Press, Chicago, Illinois; the Clarendon Press, Oxford, London, England; Methuen and Co., Ltd., London, England.

List of Illustrations

Introduction

There have been many books about Ancient Egypt but, to my knowledge, no one has yet written one which deals exclusively with the warrior kings who made Egypt great. Admittedly there is the difficulty that no one wrote their biographies and they have left no personal records, only the sometimes pompous official descriptions of campaigns inscribed on temple walls by scribes, or on stela (inscribed stones) set up by these fighting kings to mark important events in their careers.

Nevertheless, in researching other books I have been struck by the amount of interesting and sometimes dramatic material which *is* available, especially in the tombs of old soldiers who served under such monarchs as Tuthmosis I, II and III, and who wrote about them in a freer, more human way than the official chronicles would permit. There is also one's imagination, a tool to be used very cautiously when writing about the remote past. But if one has had the good luck to visit Egypt on many occasions, to see the tombs of these Pharaohs, to gaze on their mummified faces in the Cairo Museum, and even to retrace their tracks in the mountains and deserts of the Lebanon, Jordan, Syria and Iraq, they can become very real indeed.

Having decided to attempt this book, the question remained: How was one to approach the subject? By a 'semi-fictional' method padding out or 'interpreting' the few sparse facts with speculation and dramatized incidents? Or by letting the ancient documents speak largely for themselves, only adding enough to make them intelligible, and relate them to Egyptian civilization as it is known from other sources? In the end I decided on the second method, because long experience has taught me that whereas one can sometimes persuade a few people to accept 'imaginative reconstruction' in which one part fact is diluted with nine parts imagination, most readers usually like to know the facts. They have sufficient imagination, anyway, to fill in the background for themselves. And they tend to ask one the sources of one's information. How do you know this? Where is the *proof*? It is no use asking them to take one's word for it.

This is not to despise imagination, the rich flower which grows from the seed of fact; but it is necessary not only to state the fact but show where one obtained it. But, of course, it does not mean that a statement on an Ancient Egyptian monument is necessarily and entirely true. This is where scholarly interpretation helps to keep one on the rails, for the Egyptians were as much given to exaggeration, and as much likely to make mistakes, as we are. Therefore in writing this book I have drawn liberally on the researches of such scholars as the late Sir Alan Gardiner – my old friend and mentor – also Professor James Breasted, Professor Walter B. Emery, and Dr. R. O. Faulkner, whose researches into the organization of the Ancient Egyptian army are invaluable to anyone tackling this subject.

Finally there is the difficult problem of deciding where to end one's story; what to put in and what to leave out, since it is obviously impossible, in a book of this length, to describe the achievements of every Warrior Pharaoh from the First Dynasty (*c.* 3200 BC) down to the Thirty-first Dynasty (*c.* 385 BC). In the end I decided to begin with the first great Pharaoh who united Egypt by conquest, Hor-Aha (probably Menes) in about 3200 BC and end with the victory of Ramesses III over the invading 'Sea-Peoples' and their allies in about 1174 BC. There were many bitter struggles after that, and a number of valiant warrior kings. But in the writer's view the triumph of Ramesses III over an enormous coalition of invaders determined to destroy and then settle in Egypt marks the peak of successful Egyptian resistance. After that hard-won victory there was a slow but certain decline in Egypt's fortunes, with several foreign occupations, Nubian, Babylonian, Assyrian, Persian, culminating in absorption of Egypt into the empire of Rome.

The period I have chosen for my canvas covered more than 2,000 years, four times as long as the Roman Empire existed, and nearly ten times the life of the British Empire. During those twenty centuries, despite civil war and foreign invasion, Egypt maintained her unique civilization intact; it survived the collapse of the Old Kingdom in 2270 BC; it rose again during the Middle Kingdom (2100–1700 BC) and when, in about 1700 BC, it suffered the humiliation of foreign occupation for 150 years, once again a new race of warrior kings rose, rallied the people, and flung the hated 'Asiatics' out. Then followed a period, first of revival, and then of imperial glory in which Egypt became for the first and last time what we call a 'world power', with all its responsibilities, dangers and frustrations. And when the third great attack came during the reign of Ramesses III the country was equal to the challenge, and apart from very brief occupations by the Assyrians and Babylonians, the Nile Valley remained free of foreign domination until the coming of the Persians in 525 BC.

It is an exciting and inspiring story, and one which may still have lessons for us today.

LEONARD COTTRELL

Sevenhampton Manor
Near Cheltenham
Gloucestershire

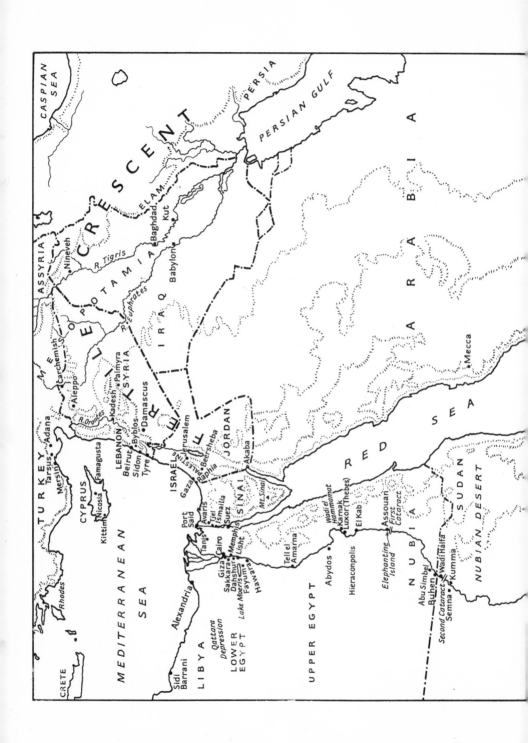

1 The Fighting Hawk

It is sometimes said that, compared with the Greeks and the Romans, the Ancient Egyptians were not a warlike people, and that is why we do not normally associate them with military skill and valour. But this attitude is largely due to ignorance and perhaps some prejudice. Over a period of about 2,000 years the Egyptians produced a number of magnificent fighting generals whom we have called the 'Warrior Pharaohs'. And while it may be true that some peoples are better at soldiering than others, for example the Sikhs and the Ghurkas in comparatively recent times, it is equally true that, given the cause, the leadership and the inspiration, peoples who are normally peace-loving can become valiant soldiers. Throughout much of their history the Ancient Egyptians enjoyed peace and were not interested in war. But when the challenge came they rose to it, as when they were occupied for 150 years by foreign invaders whom they despised.

The Romans, in later centuries, faced similar challenges. At first they were a group of peaceful farmers who had settled on the Seven Hills near the river Tiber, but determined to protect their land from their much more powerful neighbours, the Etruscans, who controlled most of what is now Italy. Having, over long and bitter years of struggle, defeated the Etruscans, they were faced with other foes and, in the end, had to conquer the whole of Italy. Even this was not the end of their problems. The newly established Roman state had come into contact with other powers, notably that of Carthage, which, jealous or afraid of the Romans, sought to crush them. So the Romans, too, had to learn the art of naval warfare, using their fleet to transport their soldiers to distant shores such as those of Britain, Syria and North Africa. In the end they became masters of most of the known world; they created an empire in which peoples of many diverse nations were absorbed into one unified system governed from Rome, linked by splendid roads, policed and protected by the Roman Army, the finest in the world. Yet all this began quite simply when a small group or tribe, speaking the Latin language, occupied a piece of land no larger then, say, the County of Warwickshire in England, fought to defend it, and then spread far beyond its borders.

We have to look at the Ancient Egyptian fighting-man against a completely different background. The civilization of Ancient Egypt, which lasted for some 3,000 years, developed in an area which, throughout much of its existence, was protected from the attacks of powerful enemies. When these attacks came they were sudden, violent and dramatic. But for most of those 3,000 years or more the Ancient Egyptians were isolated in a way that the Greeks and Romans were not. It is important to understand how and why this happened if we are to see the Warrior Pharaohs in their true perspective.

Egypt is like no other land in the world. There are no great mountains; there are no great plains; there are no green fields, except along a narrow strip some 700 miles long, but rarely more than a few miles broad, bordering the river Nile. And there is hardly any rain. In fact, without the Nile, Egypt would not exist at all. The Greek historian Herodotus truly said that 'Egypt is the gift of the Nile', because the wealth of Ancient Egypt lay in its fertility, and that fertility depended entirely on the great river. Every year, fed by the Great Lakes of equatorial Africa far to the south, the Nile brought down millions of tons of fertile mud scoured from the mountains of Abyssinia. This mud, borne down by the Nile's tributary, the Blue Nile, spread out across the valley during the time of the inundation. When the floods ceased and the river returned to its normal level, crops could be grown from that mud sufficient to support a large population. And every year this miraculous fertility was renewed.

It is no wonder, then, that this valley attracted human settlers from very early times, certainly as far back as 5,000 years BC and probably earlier. Men who had been accustomed to wandering in search of wild game found an abundance along the Nile valley, not only geese and other wildfowl which bred in the marshes and reed-beds, but antelopes, gazelles, hyenas and even lions – creatures which are now found only further south, in east and central Africa. There was enough food not only for man but for his beasts, so that sheep and cattle could be raised, providing further wealth. And when the first primitive farmers arrived, bringing with them the art of growing crops from seed, their crops 'brought forth an hundredfold', so fertile was the land. Most important of all, this natural wealth was so abundant and reproductive that large numbers of people could settle permanently in this one favoured area and thus civilization could take root.

The story of how this, one of the two most ancient civilizations on earth, came into being has been told in other books. Here we are concerned only with the Ancient Egyptian fighting-man; how he was recruited, disciplined and trained, the weapons and tactics he used, and particularly how he was officered and led. During the period with which this book mainly deals – roughly between 1600 and 1200 BC – the Egyptian Army was a highly organized force and it is possible to compare it in many ways with a good modern army. But it is interesting to follow briefly the stages by which it grew into such a force, with its divisions, regiments and battalions, its specialized arms, spearmen, bowmen, charioteers, etc, more than 2,000 years before the birth of the Roman Empire. And this development is linked with the growth of Egyptian civilization itself, from a scatter of independent tribes living in reed and mud huts and using primitive stone tools to the most powerful state in the world during the fifteenth and fourteenth centuries BC.

Because there are no written records earlier than about 3200 BC – when the whole of Egypt was unified under one ruler – we can only conjecture what these early tribesmen were like by a study of the objects they left behind, mainly in their tombs, and from a few crude paintings daubed on the rocks, or occasionally on scraps of pottery. They were not all of the same physical type, as is clear from their skulls preserved in the dry sand. They must have emigrated from a number of different lands and they did not all arrive at the same time. They were Neolithic peoples, that is they used stone tools and weapons; stone axes, spears and arrows tipped with sharpened stone. These weapons must have been developed first for hunting the wild animals on which these primitives partly depended for their food supply, though one may be certain that they were also used against members of rival tribes who threatened their hunting-grounds or the lands where they grew their crops and raised their cattle.

The proof of this comes not from prehistoric Egypt, that is Egypt as it was before the dawn of written records, but from certain cave-paintings in Spain put there by people at a similar level of development. The earliest of these paintings show weapons – mainly spears and arrows – used principally against animals. But in some of the later paintings men are seen firing at each other with bows and arrows. It seems highly probable that when there were only a few hunters and plenty of animals men would rarely fight each other; they needed all their skill and courage to kill the animals which – before the invention of farming – were their main source of food. But if one tribe discovered members of another tribal family poaching on its territory and therefore encroaching on its vital food supplies, one may be sure that jealousy and anger would arise. The cry would go up – 'kill the intruders!' and though every man would carry a weapon of some sort we may fairly conjecture that those who set out deliberately to stalk and kill their enemies would be youngest, fittest and bravest members of the tribe, the kind of young men who, in later, more civilized periods, would be the natural warrior groups. In time, no doubt, such young men would become almost a race apart, specialists in man-killing. And those who were more skilled in this lethal pursuit than others would become the natural leaders of the group. The women, children and men too old to bear arms would rely for their protection on these 'braves'. This is how armies may have originated.

We cannot be sure, but something of this sort seems to have happened in 'predynastic' Egypt – the Egypt which existed for many centuries before the land was ruled by dynastic Pharaohs. In those far-off days, when the early settlers were laying claim to sectors of the rich land bordering the Nile, there was no such thing as an army in the modern sense. But every fit young man who could carry a spear or shoot straight from the bow would at times be expected to play his part in protecting the tribal lands. Not only that; if there was a more attractive piece of land near by, and if the occupying tribe was weak, there would be a strong temptation to take it by force. And the reasons for these conquests were not necessarily land-hunger. Pride, and the desire for glory and prestige might impel the bolder members of a tribe to show their bravery and audacity by conquering a neighbour's territory and making it their own.

There would also be the wish to 'show off', especially to the young women of the tribe. Man is an aggressive animal. He had to develop and encourage this aggressiveness, which soldiers call 'fighting-spirit', first in order to hunt and kill animals who were often stronger – though less intelligent – than himself. The brave and skilful hunter, the man who was most successful in killing or trapping the wild animals on which the tribe depended for its existence, would gain additional power and glory if he was equally successful in protecting the tribe from its human enemies. But if in addition he and his followers were able to enlarge the tribal lands by bold, well-planned attacks on the territory of other tribes, he would become a hero, a leader, and eventually a chieftain. And a chieftain is only one step from a king.

This was probably how the first Pharaohs (kings) of Egypt came to power, by a process similar to that which has taken place in other countries. At first the country is divided between a number of independent tribes, each with its own local chieftain. From time to time these tribes fight each other for possession of land. Sometimes a group of tribes form an alliance against another group each side being led by its most capable warrior; then there might be bigger alliances, until at last the whole country is split into two rival groups, each under its military leader, who, by this time, will have acquired the status of king. Eventually comes the final 'show-down' and the victorious king becomes the ruler of the entire country. This happened in Anglo-Saxon England. But when the whole of England fell to the Norman conquerors, Wales and Scotland still remained separate for a time. Then Wales was subdued, and finally, as recently as AD 1603, James VI of Scotland became James I of England, Scotland and Wales. And he was the founder of the Stuart Dynasty.

Incidentally, James I's accession to the British throne shows another way in which an astute ruler could increase the territory over which he ruled. He did not conquer England by force of arms, but because he was the son of Mary Queen of Scots. Very often family connections, a 'dynastic marriage' gave a king the legal right to a kingdom without needing to fight for it. Queens and princesses have, therefore, often done as much as armies could do to increase the power of kings. It is important to bear this in mind when we consider the history of Egypt and her Warrior Pharaohs.

In Ancient Egypt, between about 5000 BC and 3200 BC, we can safely assume that a similar process took place; there would be wars between rival tribes along the 700-mile length of the river; there would be conquests of weaker units leading to alliances between groups or federations under stronger leaders; also there would inevitably be improvements in the art of war. But in case the reader thinks that this is pure guesswork, let us look at the facts which lead us to this conclusion.

Archaeologists sometimes use the phrase 'the historical horizon', meaning the point in time at which written records begin. Imagine you are on a hilltop gazing across a vast tract of country. The rim of the sky, where it meets the land on the horizon, represents the point at which men began writing down what they had achieved. From that horizon to the place on which you stand it is possible to know about your ancestors from written records, however sparse and imperfect they may be. But beyond the horizon lies what? Emptiness, a mere void? By no means. If you travel towards the horizon, you will find, stretching before you, more and more land, going on and on to infinity. Men occupied this territory, too, in times long past; they hunted animals, grew crops, begot children, perhaps built cities and made war on their neighbours. But they had not yet learned to write, so there is no way of knowing who they were and what they did *except for the articles they left behind in the earth*. This is how we know a little about the so-called 'predynastic' people who occupied the Nile Valley for some 2,000 years before the first Pharaoh reigned over it.

However, there is another way we can know something about them, and that is by looking backward at them through the eyes of their successors, the 'dynastic' peoples who *could* write. From about 3200 onwards, when the first known Pharaoh of the First Dynasty reigned over a united Egypt, the Ancient Egyptians kept written records. At first these were very crude and primitive; a few scrawls painted on rocks overlooking the river, in caves, on scraps of pottery. Later, as the skill of the artists improved, they left written records and pictures carved on stone. Still later the scribes – the literate men who had mastered the art of writing – used a more convenient though less durable material called papyrus, a kind of paper manufactured from the pith of the papyrus plant which grew in abundance beside the Nile. Thousands, perhaps millions, of these papyrus scrolls must once have existed. But most have perished long ago. However, thanks to the dry climate of Egypt, and the Egyptian custom of putting papyrus scrolls in tombs, a few examples of these precious records have survived, together with the much more numerous inscriptions carved on the walls of temples and tombs. From these records, set down in a dead language which was only deciphered about 150 years ago, we can learn a great deal about the Pharaohs of the dynastic period (from 3200 BC down to about 332 BC), and a little concerning their primitive tribal ancestors, the Stone Age people who occupied the Nile Valley for thousands of years before the days of the mighty pyramid-builders, when the Pharaohs ruled over a huge united kingdom, built cities and temples of hewn stone or mud-brick, buried their dead in magnificently furnished tombs, and commanded fleets and armies which won for them a great empire.

Among the earliest records which have come down to us is an extraordinary document dating from about 3200 BC called the Palette of Narmer. It can be seen in the Petrie Collection at University College, London, and is reproduced, in (Plates 3 and 4). Another equally precious record is known as the Mace-Head of

Hieraconpolis (Plate 5). They should be studied together. I have used the word 'precious' because, just as a rare diamond is more valuable than gold and silver, so these objects, small and relatively crude though they appear, are more valuable to archaeologists than many of the much more elaborate and huge monuments of the later Pharaohs. Why? For the same reason that a letter from Thomas Jefferson is more valuable than one from President Johnson, or a document signed by King Alfred the Great is of greater interest than one bearing the signature of Queen Elizabeth II. Because the Narmer palette and the Hieraconpolis Mace-Head take us back to the very beginning of Ancient Egyptian civilization; and, moreover, they tell us something of what took place long before Narmer, the first known Pharaoh, was born.

We will look first at the ceremonial palette of King Narmer. We call it a 'ceremonial' palette because it had no practical purpose. It is much too large for grinding paint on, but it had its origin in much smaller stone palettes found in predynastic tombs which did serve this purpose. The paint, incidentally, was green malachite and was used for painting the eyelids, probably as a protection against the sun's glare. The ceremonial palette might be compared with the huge mace which is kept in the House of Commons; originally the mace was a weapon of war, but even the most angry Member of Parliament would not pick up the ceremonial mace to fell his opponent!

On this palette King Narmer showed several important scenes which he wished to commemorate. They all symbolize victory in battle. On one side (Plate 3) we see the warrior king wearing the tall head-dress which symbolized his rule over Upper (i.e. southern) Egypt. In his right hand he grasps a club or mace, while with his left he grasps the hair of a bearded man who sprawls abjectly on the ground. Behind the king, but represented much smaller, is a figure which may depict the Pharaoh's page, carrying his sandals, and in front of Narmer, above the figure of the captive, is a falcon standing above another prostrate figure to the nose of which is attached a rope which the bird is holding. The hawk is Horus, the falcon-headed god of Hieraconpolis, from which Narmer came, and the bearded, prostrate figure represents a conquered king of

Lower (i.e. northern) Egypt – the Delta region which borders on the Mediterranean.

Now notice the two running men at the bottom of the palette; they represent the king's enemies, in flight. And the little rectangle above the left-hand running fugitive appears to show a fortress (a plan view) which the victorious Narmer had overthrown. Another fortress is indicated at the bottom of the other side of the palette (Plate 4), this time with curving walls set with projecting towers (as seen from the top). The figure of the bull with lowered horns, breaking down the walls, again symbolizes the Pharaoh, one of whose titles was 'Mighty Bull'. Below him is another running man.

The middle part of this scene, showing two strange animals with long, linked necks, each tethered by a rope to a human figure, is not easy to understand, though some believe it symbolizes the capture by Narmer of the two kingdoms of Upper and Lower Egypt, but the meaning of the uppermost scene, below the twin bulls with human faces, is quite clear. On the left, followed by his page, is Narmer again, this time wearing the crown or head-dress of Lower Egypt. In front march his standard-bearers, and in front of them lie the headless bodies of slain enemies. But notice also the boat with high prow and stern above the bodies, and, here and there, hieroglyphic signs which give us the name Narmer and clues to the meaning of the scenes. For by this time Ancient Egypt had taken a big step forward on the road to civilization, the invention of writing.

Now look at the Hieraconpolis Mace-Head (Plates 5 and 6). Here again we see King Narmer wearing the red crown of the conquered North, with his standard-bearers. He is seated, and in front of him is a figure, also seated, under a palanquin or canopy, behind which bearded men march, and behind them, at a lower level, is a crouching bearded figure who appears to have his hands bound behind his back. If you look carefully, you will observe that Narmer's throne is at the top of a flight of steps and below him stand two fan-bearers carrying ostrich-feather fans; both these details are put there to emphasize his dignity and importance. But who is the little seated figure facing him under the canopy? It is generally believed that this represents a woman, probably a princess of the captured Northern Kingdom whom Narmer is about to marry in order to make good his claim to the throne. Martial conquest was probably not enough. The right to inherit the throne of Egypt was through the female line. You became a Pharaoh if you married the widow or heiress of the previous Pharaoh. Some Egyptologists think that this little princess was named Nithotep, whose ruined tomb has been discovered south of Nagadeh, in Upper Egypt.

These two objects, the Palette of Narmer and the Mace-Head, both appear to commemorate a victory of the King of Upper Egypt over his Lower Egyptian rivals. Lower or northern Egypt, where the wide, fertile delta fans out from a point just north of modern Cairo, was the richest land in Egypt. Probably also the people of Lower Egypt were more civilized than those of the south; in fact, there is evidence to suggest that it was they who invented writing. We do not know whether this tough fighting Pharaoh from the south was the man who finally brought Egypt under one united rule or whether he or his successor Aha was the King Menes whom the later Egyptians regarded as the first king of the First Dynasty. But he undoubtedly defeated the northerners in a great battle which brought him rich plunder.

Look again at the Mace-Head (Plate 6) and notice, in the centre beneath the figures of the marching men, pictures of an ox, a goat, and a man with upraised arms. The signs under these figures tell us that Narmer claims to have captured 120,000 men, 400,000 oxen and 1,422,000 goats. An exaggeration, perhaps – the Pharaohs were given to boasting – but one may be sure that the king had something to boast about.

His successor was named Hor-Aha, which means 'Fighting Hawk' and some scholars believe that he was the first unifier of Egypt, the founder of the First Dynasty. One of his names – the Pharaohs always bore several – was *Men*, which may mean 'established', and it was most probably this king, and not Narmer, to whom the later Egyptian historians gave the Greek name *Menes*. The two names, Hor-Aha and Men, appear on an ivory label discovered in the great tomb of the king's mother Nithotep. And the distinguished British archaeologist Professor Garstang discovered in the same tomb another ivory label bearing the scene reproduced in Plate 2.

It is worth studying in detail, although the art may strike you as primitive. But at this period, more than 400 years before the building of the first pyramid, the Egyptians had not learned to fashion huge stone buildings and adorn them with monumental sculpture. Already, however, we can see the representations of the animal-headed gods and goddesses which become so familiar in later Pharaonic times. Notice on the right, for example, three marching figures with animal heads, including the lioness-headed goddess; and near the top, on the right-hand side, is the falcon-god Horus, the principal deity of Hieraconpolis, the capital, for a time, of these conquering southern Pharaohs. Notice particularly the two human figures facing each other near the centre. According to Professor W. B. Emery, 'this scene appears to represent some ceremony commemorating the Unification of the Two Lands, represented by two human figures performing some function over an unidentified object – the ceremony was called 'Receiving the South and the North'[1] – as the hieroglyphs tell us.

This unifying of the entire land of Egypt, from the Mediterranean Sea to the First Cataract, is of immense importance, because it marked the end of one stage in Egypt's development and the beginning of another. For 2,000 years or perhaps more the inhabitants of the Nile Valley had lived, first as independent tribes, then in larger units composed of several tribes under powerful leaders, each with its own local gods and goddesses. Throughout that enormous stretch of time, despite intertribal wars and conquests, there was co-operation between these peoples. There had to be because of the river. It was a mighty thoroughfare uniting the land, and its annual flooding – the source of Egypt's wealth – forced the tribes to co-operate in flood control, the building of embankments and irrigation ditches, and the measurement of the Nile's annual rise, since a 'low Nile' could mean a bad harvest and the need to store grain against famine, whereas a 'high Nile' meant excessive flooding and perhaps the wiping out of land boundaries.

This need for total control of the kingdom – unlike the situation in Greece, where tribes could and did live independently – did more than anything to shape Egyptian civilization, including the Pharaonic armies. The Egyptians became accustomed, from very early days, to the strong leadership of one man, the type of government which nowadays we call 'authoritarian' and which the Ancient Greeks would call 'tyrannical'. They were never a free people who could choose their leaders and get rid of them when they wished. They were used to unquestioning obedience to their ruler and his high officials, who could call upon them not only to go to war but dig ditches and build embankments to control the floods, and later to build the mighty pyramids and temples which still astonish us today.

They obeyed their kings not only because they were powerful monarchs with armies and police at their command – let alone tax-collectors – but, more important, because they regarded these rulers as gods, and the sons of gods. This may not be easy to understand nowadays when the worship of God is something quite separate. We do not think of a president, a king or a queen as the direct descendant of the Almighty. In Ancient Egypt kings were remote from the common people, surrounded by pomp and magnificence, served by troops of courtiers and magnificently robed officials bearing high-sounding titles such as 'fan-bearer on the Right Hand of His Majesty'.

The ordinary Egyptian man or woman was taught to believe that their kings were descended, not from mortal beings like themselves, but from the great gods and goddesses who made the world; deities such as the falcon-god Horus of Hieraconpolis, Ptah of Memphis, and Osiris, God of the Dead. They also believed that their kings, like the gods, were immortal, and that when they ceased to live on earth they continued to rule from the sky. This was why the Egyptians laboured to erect enormous tombs called pyramids, the eternal resting-places of their god-kings. Such beliefs were rarely questioned, because the priests, who controlled the schools and seats of higher learning, said so.

We have grown accustomed to thinking of Ancient Egyptian civilization in these terms, as something complete and accomplished; the divine Pharaoh ruling from his palace, the pyramids pointing into the blue sky, the huge stone-built temples and tombs, the rich, gold-encased funerary equipment of such a king as Tutankhamun. And if we think of the Pharaoh's armies we probably imagine ranks of disciplined soldiers marching in step, armed with swords, spears and shields, or riding in chariots, as we have seen them in tomb-models and tomb-paintings and sculptured reliefs. But all these things had to have a beginning, and that beginning seems to have been with Hor-Aha, 'the Fighting Hawk', who unified the Two Lands and built his capital at Memphis, at the point where the Nile Valley broadens out into the fertile Delta to the north. But behind Hor-Aha stretch centuries of slow development; from the primitive Stone Age settlers living in reed-huts beside the Nile to the Bronze Age men who had learned to fuse copper and tin to make more durable weapons; from a scatter of independent tribes frequently at war with each other to two strong kingdoms which finally became one united Egyptian state.

By about 3200 BC the Ancient Egyptians had already acquired most of the arts of civilization; they had long ceased to be barbarians. Although they had not yet learned to build monumentally in stone, they could build splendid tombs for their kings and queens in mud-brick, with stone-lined burial chambers and store-rooms stacked with rich furniture, in ebony, ivory and gold. They were skilful shipbuilders and seafarers, too, trading not only up and down the Nile Valley but out across the Mediterranean to the Lebanon, from which they obtained their tall masts. They could read and write, and keep records in their newly invented writing system.

But such wars as they had fought had been within their own country. They had no rivals of equal power. No newcomers had yet threatened them with superior weapons and fighting skill. The Nubians to the south were a Negroid people at a much lower level of development, who sometimes caused trouble but could be controlled. To east and west of the Valley lay empty desert, harsh and sterile, hemming the Egyptians in, but providing a natural protection against invasion. West of the Delta lived the desert-dwelling Libyans who, like the Nubians, could sometimes be a nuisance, but never a serious threat. As for the peoples of western Asia, who lived near the coasts of what are now the Lebanon, Syria and Israel, they were organized in tribes who provided a valuable source of trade, but who offered no military threat. This happy situation was to continue for at least another 1500 years.

As for the 'Fighting Hawk', we know very little, apart from what was recorded by the Greek historian Diodorus the Sicilian, who visited Egypt in the first century BC, some 3,000 or more years after the reign of Aha (whom Diodorus called Menes). The Greek traveller had never heard of Aha by his Ancient Egyptian name, or seen his tomb; nor could he read the ancient writings which archaeologists have deciphered in comparatively recent times. But he did have access to the priestly histories of Egypt's ancient kings. And what the priests told him was this; that Aha was a mighty hunter, and that when he was pursuing game in the Fayum Oasis he was treacherously attacked by his hounds and only escaped by leaping into Lake Moeris. Diodorus also tells us that this king was the first to teach the Egyptians the arts of civilization and how to worship the gods. His death, it is said, was brought about through injuries he received while hunting the hippopotamus.

There is one final point concerning Hor-Aha, his predecessor Narmer and the rulers who came before them. Were they of native Egyptian stock, as used to be believed; or were they of foreign origin? It is certainly curious that, after a couple of thousand years of apparently tranquil development, Ancient Egypt suddenly produces rulers who are capable of such extraordinary feats, unifying the entire land and creating monumental tombs to protect their bodies after death.

Professor Walter Emery, who has spent many years investigating the tombs of these kings of the so-called 'Archaic Period', strongly believes that they originated outside Egypt.

Emery advances a number of reasons for his belief. He points out that there are remarkable resemblances between 'archaic' Egyptian art and that of Sumer, the ancient civilization which grew up in lower Mesopotamia in the fourth millennium BC. Take, for instance, the two long-necked animals on the Narmer palette and compare them with those shown in Plate 7, which comes from Mesopotamia. Then there is the famous knife-handle from Gebel-el Arak in Egypt (Plates 8 and 9), which shows typical Egyptian ships in conflict with strange vessels with very high prows and sterns. It seems to depict a battle at sea against invaders; but if you look carefully at the figure at the top of Plate 9, holding apart two lions, and compare it with a similar figure illustrated in Plate 10, from Sumer, the similarity is obvious.

This in itself does not prove that the founders of Egyptian civilization – the 'Sons of Horus', as they were called – were necessarily foreigners, though there is no doubt that the Egyptians of the late predynastic and early archaic periods were influenced by the art of Sumer. Besides the examples I have quoted there is the striking similarity between what are called 'panelled-façade' buildings in Egypt and similar buildings in Mesopotamia. Also it is now certain that the Egyptian writing system, the 'hieroglyphs', borrowed certain signs from Sumer. But such resemblances may merely show that the two peoples were in contact, not that one conquered the other.

On the other hand, as Emery points out, 'graves of the late predynastic period in the northern part of Upper Egypt were found to contain the anatomical remains of a people whose skulls are of greater size and whose bodies were larger than those of the natives, the difference being so marked that any suggestion that these people derived from the earlier stock is impossible'.[2] The Professor is persuasive, and his theory is tempting; but a large number of Egyptologists have yet to be convinced, although some will readily admit that there may have been a gradual filtering into Egypt of peoples whose civilization was more advanced. They may have entered the Nile Valley via the Wadi-el-Hammamat in Upper Egypt, which links the Upper Nile with the Red Sea. Or they could have entered by a northerly route via the Wadi-el-Tumilat on the east side of the Delta (see map, page 4). If these 'Sons of Horus' were, in fact, foreign invaders who imposed their rule on the early Egyptians as the Normans conquered the Anglo-Saxons, they were the last to do so for some 1500 years. Throughout those fifteen centuries, from the First Dynasty down to the seventeenth, Egypt was not threatened from beyond her borders. The wars which she fought were frontier wars, against the Nubians in the south and the Libyans in the west. Any other conflicts were within Egypt herself.

---

[1] Emery, W. B., *Archaic Egypt*, Penguin Books, 1961
[2] Emery, W. B., op. cit.

2 'A Mighty Man of Valour'

In Ancient Egypt there were what we would call 'professional soldiers', that is, men whose trade was soldiering. As youngsters they were taught to bear arms, to march in step, to obey the commands of their officers, to fight with the spear, sword and bow. But there were others, usually men of good families, who exercised these skills in an amateur way, for the fun of it. Most young Egyptians were accustomed to hunt wild game, and proficiency in killing beasts is not far removed from fighting one's fellow men. In each case steadiness of nerve, courage, marksmanship and physical agility are important.

There was a man called Sinuhe who lived more than a thousand years after Hor-Aha – the 'fighting hawk' conquered Egypt. He was not a Pharaoh, though he probably came of royal blood, since in his day high officials were often drawn from members of the royal family. And Sinuhe (pronounced Sin-*ewe*-ee) was evidently a very important official, known personally to the King and Queen. But this is not the main reason why we should look at him closely. Doubtless there were many Sinuhes – 'mighty men of valour' – during the thirty generations who lived between 3200 BC and about 1890 BC, when the Sinuhe of our story was alive. But it happens that Sinuhe's adventures were recorded, by himself, in such interesting detail that we feel almost as if we knew him personally.

When the story opens he is serving as an officer in the army of Amenemhat II which has been sent to punish the Tjemeh (Libyans) of the western desert. These, together with the Nubians of the south, were traditional enemies of Egypt. The Libyans looked with envy at the rich land of the Delta, from which perhaps their remote ancestors had been evicted by Narmer, Hor-Aha and the founding Pharaohs of the First Dynasty, and from time to time they made war on the Egyptians, raiding across the frontier and stealing cattle. They wore tall head-dresses and long robes, unlike the Egyptians, who wore a short kilt-like garment. (A few years ago, when the late Zakaria Goneim dug out a wall at Sakkara dating from about 2700 BC, I remember seeing a crude drawing of a Libyan in his long robe and tall hat, put there by one of the workmen in an idle moment nearly 5,000 years ago.)

It so happened that Sinuhe, who when the story opens was still a youth, did most of his fighting among Bedouin tribesmen, and not in the ranks of the Egyptian Army. The reason was that when the royal army was returning to the capital, driving before it thousands of Libyan captives, the old Pharaoh Amenemhat II died. His son, Senusret, was in command of the armed forces and apparently Sinuhe overheard a remark passed by one of the Court Officials which alarmed him. Why he was alarmed is not clear, but evidently he decided it was unsafe for him to return. When a Pharaoh died there was frequently intrigue over the succession. Perhaps Sinuhe overheard details of a plot to kill him. Perhaps he remembered the unsuccessful plot to kill one of the Pharaoh's ancestors, Amenemhat I, who wrote in a letter to his son;

> It was after supper when night was come. I took an hour of repose, lying upon my bed. I was tired and my heart began to follow sleep. Of a sudden weapons were brandished and there was talk concerning me, whilst I remained like a snake of the desert. I awoke to fight, being by myself. I found it was an attack by the guard. Had I hastened with weapons in my hand, I could have driven back the caitiffs. But there is none strong at night. None can fight alone. There is no successful issue without a protector.[1]

But Sinuhe could and did fight alone, more than once. First, however, he had to escape from Egypt by a secret route, avoiding the cities and river crossings, skirting the frontier posts where guards stood watch, and where patrols would be active; aware that once his absence from the camp was noticed armed men would be sent in pursuit.

He begins by telling us the date of the event 'Year 30' (that is the thirtieth year of the King's reign) the seventh day, 'in the third month of the inundation season' (the time of the Nile's flooding, in the autumn). News reached him that the old Pharaoh had died, that the Residence, the royal palace, was hushed, and hearts were in mourning. 'The courtiers crouched head on lap, and the nobles grieved.' The Pharaoh's eldest son, Senusret, had been sent at the head of an army to fight the tribe called the Tjehnu, who lived on the edge of the Egyptian Delta, and when the news arrived Senusret was already returning in triumph with many prisoners and cattle. Messengers arrived from the Court to inform Senusret, and met him on the road, at night. Senusret, who was next in line for the throne, lost no time, says Sinuhe. 'Not a moment did he linger, the Falcon (that is the young prince) flew off with his followers, not letting his army know.' Then follows a passage which it is difficult to understand. Sinuhe says, 'But the king's children who had accompanied him in this army had been sent for and one of them had been summoned.'

In other words there were other royal princes in that army besides Senusret and evidently a dispute had arisen. For some reason which we cannot fully understand Sinuhe felt himself dangerously involved in this; perhaps there was a plot to replace Senusret the rightful heir to the throne, with another prince, and Sinuhe may have known about this.

Without further explanation Sinuhe tells us how he determined to take flight, though at first he probably did not intend to leave Egypt but only to find a hiding-place until the trouble – whatever it was – blew over. The army had been campaigning in the desert to the north-west of the Delta (see map, page 4) and the fugitive's plan was to strike southward until he could cross from the west to the east bank of the Nile at a point affording a swift passage.

He set out southward, he tells, but without intending to reach the 'Residence', that is the capital city, because he expected there would be trouble there following the sudden death of the Pharaoh. He also gives us details of his route. He crossed 'Lake Ma'aty near Sycamore' and then came upon what the manuscript calls 'Snofru Island'. Now, Snofru was the name of a great Pharaoh of the Fourth

Dynasty whose pyramid still stands, and it has been suggested by one authority that it is this great monument which is meant. Snofru's pyramid is near the edge of the cultivated land on the edge of the western desert, west of the Nile, which Sinuhe knew he must cross. So, until he could steal a boat, he spent the day 'on the edge of the fields'. At one point a man spotted him, staring at the stranger for a while, but, says the fugitive, 'he stood in awe of me and was afraid'. Probably Sinuhe threatened him, and he went away.

When evening came Sinuhe came near to a place called Oxtown, where he 'crossed over in a barge without a rudder, by the aid of the west wind'.

Although these names are no longer used in modern Egypt, it is possible to follow Sinuhe's route with some accuracy, even to-day. It seems reasonable to believe that he stole a boat somewhere near Dashur, well south of the great city of Memphis, which he would naturally wish to avoid. That he stole the boat is likely on several counts; first he would not wish to be seen by a boatman, and second, because the boat he used was 'a barge without rudder'. To this day the Egyptian boatmen, when mooring their craft for the night, often take away the rudder as a precaution against thieves. So Sinuhe was unlucky. Instead of a swift sailing-boat or rowboat he had to push out into the northward-flowing river in a clumsy old barge without means of steering, and rely on the current to take him across. But by the time the barge reached the eastern bank it had carried him miles downriver to a point which nowadays is near the centre of modern Cairo. This seems pretty certain, because Sinuhe goes on to tell us that he 'passed by the east of the quarry above the Mistress-of-the-Red Mountain'.

To this day one can still see these ancient Egyptian quarries in the red sandstone cliffs high above the modern capital of Egypt. In fact, I have attempted to follow the early part of Sinuhe's route myself and it was exciting to recognize the same landmarks, the pyramid of Snofru at Dashur, the quarries in the Red Mountain, just as they were 4,000 years ago.

But having been carried so far northward Sinuhe had to abandon his plan of going south. Instead he struck out in the direction of the Sinai Desert and the north-easterly frontier of his native

The ivory label discovered in the tomb of Queen
Nithotep   *Penguin Books*

Reconstruction drawing of the Mace-Head by Professor Emery. Notice king
under canopy and figure of seated princess   *Penguin Books*

A seal from Sumer   *The Mansell Collection*

The palette of Narmer. The warrior king is wearing the tall head-dress
which symbolized his rule over Upper Egypt   *Roger Wood*

The carved ivory handle of the knife from Gebel-el-Arak   *Roger Wood*

Serpent-necked felines on palette from Mesopotamia   *Ashmolean Museum*

land. Now truly he was a fugitive; there was no going back, and ahead of him, beyond the frontier posts guarded by Pharaoh's troops, lay a hostile, almost waterless land peopled by fierce Bedouin tribes, the 'Sand-dwellers' as the civilized Egyptians called them, 'their hearts not mild'.

He hurried northward as fast as his feet would carry him, reaching a frontier fortress called 'Wall of the Ruler'. There he had to crouch for hours hidden behind a bush lest the watchmen on the battlements should see him. At night he was able to avoid being seen, crossed the frontier and made his way into the pitiless desert beyond, 'the land of the Sand-dwellers'. The journey was a terrible one, for the days are blindingly hot, and unless one knows the tracks leading to the oases – the desert springs, which are rare – one can die agonizingly of thirst. And the young courtier-soldier, used to the civilized life of the Egyptian Court, did not know them well. But he managed to reach two places which he evidently knew, the 'Island of Kem-War' and a place called Peten. At Kem-War he was at the point of collapse. In his own words:

An attack of thirst overtook me. I was parched, and my throat was dusty. I said; 'this is the taste of death!' But then I lifted up my heart and collected myself, for I had heard the sound of the lowing of cattle, and I spied Asiatics. The Sheikh among them, who had been in Egypt, recognized me. Then he gave me water while he boiled milk for me. I went with him to his tribe. What they did (for me) was good.[2]

To anyone who has travelled in Egypt and its desert borderlands the fascination of this passage is that it might have been written only yesterday. Today, although there are metalled motor-roads across the Desert of Sinai, if one's vehicle breaks down and one strays a few hundred yards into the sand-dunes one might well be Sinuhe, wandering, weak and parched by thirst, with the vultures circling overhead. And then the relief at 'hearing the lowing of cattle' and to come upon the black tents of the Bedouin Arabs, the same 'Asiatics' whom Sinuhe knew, wearing the same long robes, driving their sheep and goats from one oasis to the next. We, too, would be as grateful as he was for the rasp of cool water on the tongue, and the sour goats' milk. . . . 'What they did for me was good . . .'

The friendly Sheikh, 'who had been in Egypt', evidently provided guides for the young man, for Sinuhe confidently says that
'One foreign country gave me to another' as he passed oasis to
oasis, always moving northwards to what are now the countries
of the Lebanon, Israel and Syria. 'I set off for Byblos and approached Qedem, and spent a year and a half there.' The ruins of
Byblos can still be visited a few miles north of Beirut, capital of
the Lebanon, but the location of Qedem is uncertain. It was at this
place that Sinuhe was befriended by a local ruler named Ammi-
enshi (a Semitic name) who governed the land of Retenu (modern
Israel, Jordan and Syria).

> He set me at the head of his children. He married me to his eldest daughter.
> He let me choose for myself of his country, of the choicest of that which was
> with him on his frontier with another country. It was a good land, named
> Yaa. Figs were in it, and grapes. It has more wine than water. Plentiful was
> its honey, abundant its olives. Every kind of fruit was on its trees. Barley was
> there, and emmer (wheat). There was no limit to any (kind of) cattle. He made
> me ruler of a tribe of the choicest of his country.[3]

Now we must allow for the fact that Sinuhe was telling this
story in his old age, after he had returned to Egypt, and no doubt
distance lent enchantment to his view. But there can be little
doubt that most of what he says was true. The description of the
fertile country over part of which he ruled corresponds with much
of Israel, the Lebanon and Jordan as they are today. It was this
same land which, hundreds of years later, the Hebrew prophets
described as 'a land flowing with milk and honey'. But, unlike
the Nile Valley, it was open to attack from several sides and it
was probably this fact which led the shrewd Semitic chieftain,
Ammi-enshi, a ruler of Upper Retenu, to adopt the young
Egyptian nobleman as a son and persuade him to make his home
there.

For, Court-bred though he was, and a fugitive from his own
country, there was nothing soft about Sinuhe. He was a fighting-
man, trained to arms, and possessed of remarkable courage and
skill. Evidently he was also a capable general.

The ruler of Retenu made Sinuhe commander of his army, and
the young man excelled himself in military skill and courage. He led

campaigns against several foreign states, enemies of Ammi-enshi and – according to his own account – was invariably successful. This was desert warfare, a battle for grazing-grounds and wells and, not to put too fine a point on it, many of these battles were, nothing more than cattle-raids. 'I plundered the enemy's cattle', boasts Sinuhe, 'and slew people in it by my strong arm, my bow, my movements and by my successful plans.' One can be certain that the young Egyptian, who had been trained in civilized warfare, was a tremendous asset to his Bedouin employer. 'He loved me,' he writes, 'he recognized my valour', and he 'placed me at the head of his children'. That is to say, he honoured Sinuhe above his own warrior sons.

Sinuhe had, in fact, 'gone native', becoming like a Bedouin in his dress and manners, leading their young braves on cattle-raids, a very different Sinuhe from the elegantly dressed officer who had accompanied the Pharaoh's armies when they went to chastise the Libyans. No doubt he enjoyed it, or he would not have stayed with people whom his still looked on as barbarians. The climax of his story comes when 'a mighty man of Retenu came, that he might challenge me in my own camp. He was a hero without his peer . . . He said he would fight me, he intended to despoil me, and he planned to plunder my cattle, on the advice of his tribe.'

The story of this combat reminds one of the slaying of Goliath by David (one imagines that Sinuhe, like most Egyptians, was a small, lithe man, whereas Bedouin warriors were often over six feet tall). Quite apart from its drama the account is interesting as showing the fighting methods used. Sinuhe uses his brains as well as his muscles, whereas his opponent, to judge from this description, had more strength than cleverness.

During the night before the combat, Sinuhe tells us, he practised with his bow, polished his weapons, saw that his dagger was easy in its sheath. And when day broke he saw before him a huge concourse of the enemy tribes, led by their champion whom Sinuhe was to fight.

I had thought (only) of this fight. . . . Every heart burned for me; women and men groaned. Every heart was sick for me. They said; 'Is there another strong man who could fight against him?'

Then he took his shield, his battle-axe, and his armful of javeline. Now after I had let his weapons issue forth, I made his arrows pass by me uselessly, one close to another. He charged me, and I shot him, my arrow sticking in his neck. He cried out and fell on his nose. I felled him with his own battle-axe and raised my cry of victory over his back, while every Asiatic roared. I gave praise to Montu [Egyptian god of war], while his adherents were mourning over him. This ruler Ammi-enshi took me into his embrace. Then I carried off (the enemy's) goods and plundered his cattle. What he had planned to do to me I did to him. I took what was in his tent and stripped his encampment[4]

Two things may strike you as strange in this marvellous passage. First it is extremely boastful by our modern Western standards. We have been taught that it is in bad taste to praise oneself and crow over defeated enemies like a turkey-cock. But the Egyptians saw no shame in it, and neither did the Ancient Greeks of Homer's time – think of the boasting and bragging of Achilles in the *Iliad*. 'Other times, other manners', wrote a wise French author. And if we are to understand the fighting-men of Egypt we shall have to get used to what we regard as swank, because they all blew their own trumpets resoundingly!

The other strange passage refers to the god of war being 'assuaged', as if Sinuhe had committed some offence for which he had purged himself by his victory. What was this offence? Probably Sinuhe felt guilty at having deserted his master the Pharaoh, and felt that by being 'a good Egyptian' in a foreign land, brave and resolute in combat, he had won the god's forgiveness. He had set a good example to the 'Asiatics', had protected the land and property of his patron Ammi-enshi, and shown him how to make war successfully.

But throughout his long years of exile he pined for Egypt. He made a point of entertaining the royal messengers of the Pharaoh when they passed through Retenu. 'I used to make everybody stop over', he writes. 'I gave water to the thirsty. I put him who had strayed back on the road. I rescued him who had been robbed.' And no doubt he discussed with these messengers the latest news from the Residence. He learned that the young prince Senusret was firmly established on the throne after his father's death. Now no longer a young man, but, like Sinuhe, a middle-aged ruler with grown-up sons, he wanted to see again his old comrade-in-arms who had fled the country so many years ago. Eventually Sinuhe was convinced that it was safe for him to return to Egypt.

First he handed over his property to the children who had been born to him through his marriage with the chieftain's daughter. Knowing he would never return to 'the land of the Sand-dwellers', Sinuhe handed over to his sons his servants, cattle, fruit, and all his land.

Then, laden with gifts from his friend Ammi-enshi, and no doubt after tearful farewells to his wives and children, Sinuhe began the long journey back to Egypt. This time he did not travel the hard desert road through Sinai where he had nearly died of thirst. He made for the coast and a port to which the Pharaoh had sent an Egyptian vessel to bring him home. This time he travelled in civilized comfort, for Senusret had sent, with the ship, servants in plenty, including cooks, butlers, and serving-men, so that his meals would be suitable to a high official whom the King of Egypt wished to honour. 'Every butler was busy at his duties. When I started and set sail, the kneading and straining of beer was carried on beside me, until I had reached the town of Lisht.'[5]

If you look at the model boats illustrated in Plate 11, you will see exactly the kind of vessels in which Sinuhe travelled back to his homeland, probably from Byblos on the Lebanese coast. They are not his boats; they were made for a high official named Meket-Re who lived at the same period, and were found in Meket-Re's tomb at Thebes by H. E. Winlock of the Metropolitan Museum of Art, New York, where they are on view today. But they show you, better than any words of mine, the kind of boats which formed Sinuhe's flotilla, even to the 'kitchen-boat' in which his meals and drinks were prepared. After the years he had spent in Retenu, wearing Bedouin robes and living the life of the 'Sand-crossers', one can easily imagine his pleasure at again wearing Egyptian dress, and enjoying the civilized delights of a high official of the Middle Kingdom. Also he was getting on in years. His sword-arm was no longer as strong as it had been when he smote the mighty foeman sent to challenge him, and though his eye was still keen, perhaps he was not quite so agile as on that day when he dodged the arrows of his enemy before 'felling him with his own battle-axe'.

Eventually the ships entered the estuary of the Nile, and Sinuhe would see, with growing excitement, the familiar landmarks, the three pyramids at Giza, already 700 years old in his day, and the quarries high in the Red Mountain to the east, and the shining northern pyramid of Snofru, not far from which he had waited, at night, for a chance to steal a boat in order to cross the river to safety.

The young men and women who served him as the ship moved up the Nile were babies when he made that crossing. What did they know or care about his adventures when he, too, was a young man? It is possible that during this long journey home Sinuhe first jotted down the notes for the story which was to become a classic of Egyptian literature. We cannot be certain of this, but it seems possible. If what he wrote is his own, and not the polished version of the story by a later scribe, then Sinuhe was not only a fine soldier and general but an artist in words. I think he probably was. I also believe that he played a trick on Senusret when he arrived at the Court. The story makes it clear that Sinuhe arrived wearing Bedouin costume, and bearded. But is seems highly unlikely that he would not have taken the first opportunity of putting on Egyptian clothes, anointing his body with perfumed oils (as was the Egyptian custom) and shaving off is beard as soon as he reached the ship with all those willing servants sent by the Pharaoh.

But perhaps during the days and nights during which the ship was moving southward Sinuhe considered that his tale would carry more conviction, when he came to tell it at Court, if he arrived wearing the same dress which he had worn for so many years when he dwelt among the barbarous 'Asiatics'. It would be more dramatic. It would make a better story. So, I believe, Sinuhe allowed his hair to grow (perhaps, after all, he did not immediately shave his beard when he stepped on to the royal ship) and before he presented himself to Senusret and his Queen he carefully donned his Bedouin robes, and may have smeared himself with a mixture of oil and sand.

The rest of the story can be left to speak for itself.

'I was led to His Majesty who was seated upon the Great Throne in a recess of fine gold.' Like all Egyptian courtiers he had to approach the divine Pharaoh 'stretched on my belly', prostrate on the palace floor, for he was in the presence of a God-King. Moreover, Sinuhe had more than the usual fear, since he had fled from the presence of Senusret all those years ago and did not know what kind of reception he would get. 'I was caught like a man in the dark,' he tells us; 'my body was powerless.'

Yet the Pharaoh's response was kindly. Senusret told one of the courtiers to lift Sinuhe up. 'Let him speak to me,' commanded the King. Still Sinuhe was too terrified to speak, so the Pharaoh addressed him in these words: 'Behold, you are come. You have trodden the foreign countries after your flight. But now old age has come upon you.'

Then follows a passage which shows very clearly the importance the Ancient Egyptian nobleman attached to having 'a goodly burial'. Long before their deaths they began to prepare their tombs, since, according to their beliefs, the tomb was the 'Eternal Home' in which the spirit of the dead man would live for all eternity.

'It is no small matter,' said the Pharaoh,' that your corpse be properly buried. You should not be buried by bowmen' (that is, by mere Bedouin tribesmen among whom Sinuhe had spent much of his life). 'Do not remain silent any longer', the King went on. 'Speak when your name is pronounced!'

But still Sinuhe could only stumble out a few abject words, so alarmed was he that the King might still suspect him of treachery. 'What is this my lord says?' he replies. 'I would like to reply, but do not know what to say. I am afraid; there is terror in me like that I knew before my flight from Egypt. Here I am before you. May Your Majesty do with me as he pleases.'

Then comes one of those little human touches which make Egyptian literature live, like that of Homer's Greece. The Pharaoh, in order to put Sinuhe at his ease, sends for the Queen and the royal children. Sinuhe thus continues his story;

Thereupon the royal children were ushered in. Then His Majesty said to the Queen 'Here is Sinuhe, come as a Bedouin, in the dress of the Asiatics!' She gave a very great cry, and the royal children clamoured all together. Then said they to His Majesty 'It is not really he, O Sovereign!'[5]

Then His Majesty said 'It is *really* he!'

Although the ancient language and way of speech is not easy to interpret, I suspect that much of this little scene was a joke. The King and Queen make fun of Sinuhe's 'barbaric' Bedouin clothes and call him 'the sheikh Si-Mehit' and 'a goodly bowman'. They are, in fact, pulling Sinuhe's leg and he knows it.

Then they [the Queen and the royal children] brought with them their bead-necklaces, their rattles, and their *sistra* [musical instruments] and presented them to His Majesty . . . 'Loose the bow and relax the arrow' cries the Queen. . . . 'Give out goodly gift to this sheikh Si-Mehit, a bowman born in Egypt! He made a flight because of you. But he need not be afraid; the face of him who beholds your face need not blench. . . .'

The story ends with a very moving passage in which the King provides his long-lost courtier and friend with fine apartments and gorgeous clothing; a cool room with costly things of the Treasury, clothing of royal linen, myrrh and prime oil (for anointment). And Sinuhe ends his tale with these words;

My beard was shaved and my hair was combed. A load of dirt was given to the desert, and my clothes to the Sand-dwellers. I was clad in fine linen and anointed with prime oil. I slept on a bed, I gave up the sand to them who are in it, and wood-oil to him who is anointed with it. I was given a house which had a garden . . . Meals were brought to me from the palace three of four times a day, apart from that which the royal children gave, without ceasing a moment.[6]

---

[1] Gardiner, A. H., *Egypt of the Pharaohs,* Clarendon Press, Oxford, 1961
[2] Pritchard, J. B., *Ancient Near Eastern Texts,* Princeton University Press, 1965
[3] Pritchard, J. B., op. cit.
[4] Pritchard, J. B., op. cit.
[5] Pritchard, J. B., op. cit.
[6] Pritchard, J. B., op. cit.

3 The Lords of the Southern Frontier

Ancient Egyptian civilization lasted for more than 3,000 years, and during that time changed far less in its essentials than many civilizations which existed for only a fraction of that time. Take Sinuhe for instance. He lived round about 1890 BC, but if he had been born some thousand years earlier, at the time when Djoser, First King of the Third Dynasty was building the first pyramid in the world, he would still have felt at home. Egypt would have looked much the same; there would have been a Pharaoh on the throne, the same gods were being worshipped and the same language written and spoken. And if Sinuhe had lived in say 1290 BC, 600 years *after* the Pharaoh Senusret whom he had served, he would have noticed some changes, but not many. As a fighting-man the main difference he would have noted was the use of the chariot in warfare, which did not exist in his own time. But there were still archers and spearmen, and there were the same ancient enemies, the Nubians and the Libyans, plus a few more.

If you think about this it is very extraordinary indeed. Let us just go back a thousand years before our own century and imagine how a twentieth-century soldier, with his machine-guns and bazookas and tanks and missiles, would feel if he found himself serving in the ranks of one of the Saxon kings, carrying a round leather shield and a spear. I have drawn this parallel to point out the conservatism of Egyptian civilization and its resistance to change. Perhaps, though, 'resistance' is too strong a word. The Egyptians could change when they had to, as when they adopted the chariot when it had been used triumphantly against them by

Asiatic invaders. But in general they had no need to change and adapt themselves. The pioneering kings of the Archaic Period and those of the Old Kingdom which followed it had hammered the land into strong unity, given it strength and purpose, and created a way of life which suited the inhabitants of the Nile Valley. Up to about 1700 BC there were no external enemies powerful enough to threaten Egyptian civilization. Therefore it set in a mould of convention and habit, all the more rigid because it was isolated within its enfolding deserts. It knew a little of the world outside; it knew the coastal fringes of what are now the Lebanon, Israel and Syria, and to a lesser extent the high country which lies to the east of the Lebanese and Jordanian mountains; and to the south of Assouan, beyond the point where the Nile falls in a series of deep waterfalls and rapids called cataracts, the Egyptians had carved out trade-routes through Nubia (partly the modern Sudan) and southward into the little-known and mainly hostile lands bordering the Upper Nile, whose ultimate source they never discovered.

You may ask why, if Egypt enjoyed so many natural defences and was rich, it needed armed forces at all. The answer is that the Pharaohs, like all autocratic rulers, needed an army and navy to keep law and order within their territory, which was long and strung out. The army also provided guards for the royal and noble families, and ceremonial units – rather like the British Guards Regiments – to parade on royal and official occasions, resplendent in glittering uniforms. Again, the Pharaohs needed armies to police and protect their trade-routes, especially those to the south, and it is only within comparatively recent years that archaeologists have discovered and excavated a chain of huge fortresses along these routes, some as big as some of the mightiest European castles of the Middle Ages – though built more than 4,000 years ago.

Nor was there any lack of fighting experience for the keen young soldier. He did not have to spend his time on routine police duties in the provinces, or providing escorts for the king. Even before the period known as the New Kingdom (1555–712 BC), the first time when Egypt was forced to make war on powers as great as herself, there were always frontier wars to keep the army in fettle. The Egyptians were proud of the civilization which their ancestors had created and which to them was the civilized world. Like the Romans who guarded *their* empire 2,000 years later, they considered it a sacred duty to defend their frontiers against the barbarians who occasionally threatened it.

But there was another, equally familiar reason for warfare – trade expansion. For although their country was rich in natural resources such as wheat, barley, vines, cattle, and some minerals, other things had to be obtained outside its borders. It could get what it wanted from its north-eastern neighbours by peaceful trade, e.g. the tall cedars of Lebanon; but there were other products which could only be got from the dangerous, little-known territory lying to the south, along the Upper Nile. These included gold, copper, ivory, ebony and other precious woods, and what we might call 'luxury goods' such as rare animals to stock the royal zoos, and even African pygmies to entertain the Court by their dancing. They were, in fact, called 'dancing dwarfs'.

To secure these things the Egyptians made long, painful and dangerous journeys through territory inhabited by hostile tribes. One might compare this southward expansion with the exploration of the New World by European seafarers and merchant adventurers such as Cabot, Columbus, Magellan, Drake and Raleigh in the fifteenth and sixteenth centuries AD. In both cases the motive was partly trade expansion and the lust for wealth and partly sheer love of adventure and danger. And just as sixteenth-century Europe threw up brave and resolute men to dare the unknown Atlantic, so Ancient Egypt produced leaders ready to risk their lives in the unknown south for the sake of plunder, personal glory, and adventure. If all these adventurous spirits had left us records of their journeys, they would probably be as exciting as the stories of Magellan, Drake and Frobisher. Unfortunately the records are few, and those confined mainly to the tombs erected near Assouan, near the southern frontier, by the 'Barons of Elephantine' or 'The Lords of the Southern Frontier'. But by studying these, together with the mighty castles built by the Ancient Egyptians along the Upper Nile, we can get some idea of what these men were like, and the life they lived.

Before we look at these writings let us look more closely at this mysterious land beyond the southern frontier of Ancient Egypt. If you travel upriver to Assouan today, beginning at Cairo, you will pass first the splendid line of pyramids, each the tomb of a monarch of the Old or Middle Kingdoms (from 2800 to about 1700 BC), past the site of Memphis, the capital of Egypt founded by 'the Fighting Hawk' in about 3200 BC, then on past Lisht and Hawara, where the last of the seventy pyramids reared against the western horizon slips away behind. Gradually, as day follows day, the river narrows, though it remains broad and navigable up to Assouan. From time to time your modern steamer passes under iron bridges or through locks in the great dams which were thrown across the Nile in the nineteenth and twentieth centuries. These help modern Egypt to conserve its water supply, but they did not exist in Pharaonic times, so that Sinuhe, for instance, returning to the capital from the coast of Palestine, had an uninterrupted passage as he sailed up-river.

Sometimes, during your 700-mile journey southward, the desert cliffs, ochreous in colour, step forward to the river's bank; at other times they move away to the distant horizon, leaving a broad green swathe of fertile meadowland between you and them. You see, along the bank, mud-brick villages set among palm groves, and the long-robed figures of the fellahin (peasants) working in the fields, using the same or similar tools as you will see depicted on the tombs of their ancestors, 5,000 years ago. One by one the provincial cities, with their domed mosques and minarets, loom up and display themselves. Hundreds of excited children swarm down to the bank, shouting and screaming greetings, just as, no doubt, their remote ancestors greeted the glittering barges of royalty and high officials as they swept past these banks in Pharaonic times, when the boom of the great gong gave time to the sweating rowers. In Egypt, and practically nowhere else but Egypt, you have an exciting sense of reliving the distant past.

Still the river gets narrower, twisting and turning, past the gaping mouths of tombs high in the desert cliffs, the 'eternal homes' (as they were called) of officials and governors who died some forty centuries ago. In the Middle Kingdom (2100–1700 BC) these provincial governors, or 'nomarchs', were little kings, each with his own private army, rather like the barons of medieval England who, though they owed allegiance to the King, were capable of uniting to depose him and substitute another. This was the main problem of the Middle Kingdom Pharaohs such as Senusret, to regain complete control of the country and enjoy again the absolute, unchallenged power of the Old Kingdom monarchs.

'Nomarch' is a Greek word derived from 'nome'. A *nome* was a province, corresponding to the original tribal areas which existed thousands of years before Egypt was unified by Hor-Aha. Each nome had its own set of gods and goddesses, and each had its name; the 'Jackal-nome', the 'Hare-nome', the 'Elephant-nome' and so on. In England one might compare them to counties and in the U.S.A. to states. And just as, in the United States, each separate state has rights which the central government cannot override, and just as, even in England, each county has its own council and coat of arms, so in Ancient Egypt the nomes, though all professing allegiance to the reigning Pharaoh, retained some of its privileges.

And this brings us to the organization of the Egyptian armed forces, its army and navy. Originally each nome would have had its own army, which fought against those of other nomes. Then there were alliances between groups of nomes, until in the end there were two federations of the North and South. And even after Hor-Aha brought all Egypt under one rule the traditional division between North and South remained, and to the end of Pharaonic rule the kings of Egypt called themselves 'Rulers of the South and North'. During the Old Kingdom, when the monarch wished to raise an army for foreign service, he recruited it through the governors of the nomes. Each local kinglet had to provide a certain number of men for the Pharaoh's forces. And this led to difficulties.

These soldiers were usually conscripts, that is they were young men who normally worked on their lord's land, but could be armed and led by him if danger threatened. Obviously these men would feel that the main loyalty was to their local lord, and if there was a crisis of loyalty they would rather follow a leader they knew than a king they didn't know. But their main weakness, from the Pharaoh's point of view, was that they were not regular soldiers but only mustered from time to time, either to fight or to carry out what we would call public works, such as mining in the Sinai Desert, or in the alabaster quarries of Hat-nub, or to dig ditches and raise embankments when the Nile flooded.

Although there is no record of a standing, that is a regular army, during the Old Kingdom, this does not mean that it may not have existed; indeed, it probably did, since we know that the Pharaohs of the Later Middle and New Kingdoms employed regular armies, and the custom may have begun much earlier. Obviously it would be to the advantage of a monarch, claiming to rule the whole country, to have a body of troops whose loyalty was to him and not to a local lord. We know, for instance, that from very early times the kings employed Nubian troops in their armed forces. The Nubians, who inhabited the area south of the First Cataract, were not Egyptians, and are still, to this day, recognizable by their darker skin and by great stability of character. They make equally fine soldiers and fine servants, and the Ancient Egyptians were well aware of this. Above all, because the Nubians took no interest in local Egyptian rivalries and loyalties, they could be relied upon to obey orders. In more recent times one might compare them with the Ghurkas of Nepal, whom the British Army recruits to this day for their loyalty and superb fighting qualities.

Our ship passes Luxor, home of the greatest Pharaohs, who ruled from Thebes, its ancient name, for more than a thousand years after the time of Sinuhe and Senusret. But at the time of which we are writing Thebes was just another nome, ruled by local governors who buried their dead in the high cliffs to the west of the city. The glory of Thebes was yet to come. At the moment we are living in the time of Sixth Dynasty (2420–2270 BC), and we pass southwards without stopping. Still the river bends and twists, and still it narrows, but remains easily navigable. Until, after many hours of placid cruising, you sense a change. Let us imagine that we have switched from the twentieth century AD to the twentieth century BC. We are no longer in a paddle-steamer but an Ancient Egyptian sailing-barge; only now the sails have been furled and our oarsmen are pulling hard against the current. Up forward a sailor is scanning the water and shouting back commands to the steersman. The men swing their great oars in unison to the boom of a gong which hangs astern, and their bare backs gleam with sweat. We are nearing the frontier, the point at which the Nile is no longer navigable, where the river rushes past huge black boulders of Assouan granite which we must dodge.

Near by is another barge at the mast-head of which flies the banner of the Elephant-nome and its lord. The captain shouts across the racing water to our captain, and there is a flash of white teeth as he hurls back a friendly insult. It is to be a race. Both captains know that there is just one place, as we near the landing-stage, where there is room only for one vessel to pass at a time. Whoever is first to reach that narrow passage between the rocks must be the winner. Across the water we hear the chanting of the rival crew, all Nubians, as they quicken their strokes. Our men, though tired from the long upriver slog, also increase their efforts. And now there is only the roar of the river, the thresh of the oars, and the mingled chanting of the two crews, fighting the current and each other to be the first to reach Assouan.

Gradually the two boats draw nearer, until now they are neck and neck, and only a hand's breadth separates the flashing tips of the oars. On our ship all eyes – apart from those of the rowers – are on our steersman as he stands high up on the raised stern of our swift ship. We can see him looking first to the rival vessel and then to his own, measuring the distance as he leans on the huge steering-oar (rudders have not been invented). And now ahead of us rise the twin rocks between which lies our passage. We are less than fifty yards from them, and it seems that the two vessels must collide and throw us into the threshing water. The gong beats a shade faster, the oarsmen make a last effort, and inch by inch our ship draws ahead, not much, perhaps two or three feet at most, but enough. Suddenly there are two shouts, one from the steersman of our ship as he steers for the gap between the rocks, the other from the rival captain as he orders his rowers to lift their oars to allow us passage.

We shoot ahead, just missing the prow of the other ship and

shoot through the narrow channel as our men, too, raise their oars to miss the rocks on each side. A cheer goes up from our men, who look triumphantly over their shoulders at the defeated rivals. And only then, for the first time, does our steersman's stern brown face relax in a smile. He has every reason to be pleased, not only because he has beaten his rival, but because our principal passenger, a nobleman of Elephantine, has wagered him to win.

As the two ships moor alongside each other at the quay this noble passenger leaps ashore and waits while the defeated vessel ties up. After a short time Nubian guards, very smart and erect, make a gangway, and from the other vessel there steps a man of high rank, his bare breast gleaming with jewelled necklaces, his heavy black wig framing a strong, experienced face. The two nobles greet each other with an embrace, and then we are introduced to the owner of the rival ship. His name is Sabni, Chief of the Elephant-Nome and 'Lord of the Southern Frontier'. He has the bearing and manner of a king, although, in fact, he is only a frontier baron, owing allegiance to the Pharaoh Pepi II of the Sixth Dynasty. But in these days, the latter part of the Old Kingdom, the provincial governors could and did behave like minor kings.

Carrying-chairs are waiting on the bank to carry us to Sabni's official residence, a low, many-roomed building, mostly of one storey, with plastered and whitewashed walls decorated with gaily painted frescoes, with cool courtyards, ornamental pools, and flowering shrubs. Servants bustle to and fro preparing to receive their master, and the smart Nubian soldiers at the gates come to attention as we enter. There is the sound of children's voices calling excitedly in the distance, and before long Sabni's wife, with their elder sons and daughters, hurry forward to greet him. While these affectionate family rejoicings are going on, we, Sabni's guests, are led by servants to our quarters. We bathe, put on fresh clothes, and return to the main reception-room for dinner.

The meal is most appetizing and of great variety. Duck, boiled and roast, grilled lamb, fish of various kinds, and numerous fruits and vegetables. Servants wait on us at a number of small, separate tables, and offer us different kinds of wine or beer according to our taste. There is a great deal of noise, not only the chatter and laughter of our host and hostess and fellow guests, but from the 'cabaret show' which proceeds throughout the meal. There are tumblers and acrobats, male and female dancers, accompanied by drums, pipes and castanets, and at one point an elderly blind singer is led on to sing, to the accompaniment of a harp, some of the ancient songs of Egypt. These are not always melancholy or grave; there are wild war-songs chanted and danced by warriors, and love duets between girl and boy musicians.

It is difficult to believe, looking at this highly civilized, sophisticated party, and the elegant men and women in their rich dresses and jewellery, that we are on the very frontier of Egypt. Outside in the darkness, a little way to the south, lies Nubia and the barbaric lands beyond it, lands of strange, fierce animals and strange, fierce people. And beyond them, who can doubt, lies the very rim of the world, which to the Ancient Egyptians was flat.

It is only when our host Sabni, who bears the proud title of 'Caravan-Conductor to His Majesty', begins to talk of this wonderland to the south that we become suddenly aware of mystery, terror and adventure. The word 'caravan', by the way, did not mean a vehicle. A caravan was – and still is in modern Arabia – a large assemblage of men and pack-animals gathered together under the protection of a leader and his armed escort for common protection. Sabni, and his ancestors for centuries, had been such leaders, and were called 'Caravan-Conductors' because they undertook to conduct expeditions into the interior of East Africa in search of the rare and valuable products of those lands.

Sabni is a man of powerful physique, and the muscles of his bare brown arms ripple in the light of the massed lamps, as he drains his cup of wine, which is immediately refilled by a servant. It is obvious that most of his life is spent outdoors, and lines around his eyes speak of experience, cunning, and long exposure to the sun of Africa. His sons who stand near him are also strong young men who both fear and love their father. Each of the eldest has already accompanied him on an expedition. But Sabni's own father who was also a Caravan-Conductor and Governor of the Lands of the South, died on his last trip. And Sabni went down into that wild land, sought out the body of his father, and brought it all the way back to Assouan for honourable burial near the tombs of his ancestors. He is telling us about this now.

'I took a troop of my estate with me', he says, 'a hundred asses, bearing ointment, honey, clothing, oil, as presents to those countries of the Negroes. Not all of them were friendly. Sometimes we had to fight; sometimes a bribe was sufficient. But even then, as we passed through the lands of Arthet and Wawat, we kept our bows strung and our swords ready!'

'What are those lands like?' asks Sabni's youngest boy, who has not yet been out of Assouan. 'Are the people all black, like our Nubians?'

'Some are black, some not quite black, but all darker than you are, Aku.'

'And what do they fight with father?'

'Spears mainly, and some use poisoned arrows. Deadly they are. And you never see the man who's fired at you. They hide behind the river boulders, or in the trees.'

'Trees?' repeats Aku, who has never seen a tree larger than a small Egyptian sycamore.

'Yes, trees, my boy, huge trees, bigger than anything that grows in Egypt. But usually we try to keep away from the forests. At one time my men tried to chase these attackers, follow them into the forest. They never came back. The Negroes killed them.'

'Have you seen an elephant?'

'Many times, my boy, and giraffes with huge necks, like this.' Sabni stretches his arms as wide as they will go. 'But they live in the grassland.'

'What is grassland?' inquires Aku.

His elder brother intervenes. 'You ask too many questions,' he says scornfully.

'Well, have *you* seen giraffes, then?' persists the child.

'Yes, but only when the caravan was bringing them back to Egypt. But I know what grassland is like. It's – well, it's a bit like the desert; that is, it's dry most of the time, but at some times of the year rain falls, and so it isn't just bare sand; there are small trees and bushes, and green plants in clumps. And the giraffes have long necks so that they can feed from the tops of the trees and bushes.'

'I want to see giraffes and elephants. When can I go with you, father?'

'When you're old enough,' laughs Sabni, patting his son's head.

'Well, as I was saying, after many days' march, and some sailing, when we could get out canoes on the river, we found this chief of Wawat who was keeping my father's body. He was my father's friend; he had not killed him, and he killed the man who had done the deed, and most of his tribe, so they told me. Even so I had to pay him a big price before I could put my father in the coffin I had brought. And then bring him all the way back to Assouan.

'So then I buried my father in his tomb of the Necropolis; never was one of his rank so buried before. And Pharaoh honoured me. Yes, His Majesty sent me gifts; ointment, clothing, meat and fowl, and the gold of praise. *And* a rich endowment of land.'

Perhaps you are thinking that this is a made-up story, something I imagined but which never happened. Well, when you go to Assouan today ask to be shown the tombs of the Lords of the Southern Frontier, or the Barons' Tombs as they are sometimes called. If you can, take with you someone who can read the hieroglyphic inscriptions on the walls of these tombs. And there you will be shown the tomb of Sabni. It is one of the largest sepulchres at Elephantine, on the west bank of the river opposite Assouan. On one of the walls is a long description set up by Sabni nearly 5,000 year ago, telling us how he went down into East Africa to find and bring back the body of his father, whose name was Mekhu. The Egyptians always placed enormous importance on the preservation of a dead body, because if it was not so preserved, the soul, according to their belief, would perish. Mekhu's tomb is near by, but alas the precious body was stolen for the jewels which were upon it, and destroyed thousands of years ago.

There are many other inscribed tombs near by, set up by other barons and Caravan-Conductors. From these we can learn practically all that can be known about these brave and determined warrior-adventurers. There was the great Herkhuf, for instance, who lived in the reign of Merenre, third Pharaoh of the Sixth Dynasty. His titles, according to the inscriptions he set up, were 'Prince, Count, Wearer of the Royal Seal, Sole Companion, Ritual

Priest and Caravan-Conductor'. Although he held so many im-
portant-sounding titles one may be sure that he was most proud
of his prowess as Caravan-Conductor, since he devotes most of
the space to an account of his adventures in Africa.

The first account is brief. It states;

'The Majesty of Merenre, my Lord, sent me together with my
father, the Sole Companion and Ritual Priest, Iri, to Iam, in order
to explore a road to this country. I did it in only seven months, and
I brought all kinds of gifts from it. I was greatly praised for it.'

Notice that, as with Sabni, Herkhuf first gained experience of
this dangerous trade with his father Iri. But the next time he
commanded a caravan on his own, accompanied, no doubt, by
picked troops.

'His Majesty sent me a second time alone; I went forth upon the
Elephantine road, and I descended from Arthet, Mekher, Tereres,
being an affair of eight months. When I descended, I brought gifts
from this country in very great quantity. Never before was the
like brought to this land. . . .'

The word 'descended' is significant. The Ancient Egyptians,
whose country was mainly low-lying – so far as the Nile Valley
was concerned – always went 'up' out of Egypt and 'descended'
into it, whether they were returning from the southern lands of the
Upper Nile which they called Arthet, Mekher, Tereres, Wawat,
etc., or from the mountains of the Lebanon and Syria on the
north-east.

When the indefatigable Herkhuf went on his fourth expedition
he had to use diplomacy. The native chieftain of the Iam folk was
about to make war on the Libyans of the Oases – the desert-dwel-
lers living to the west. If war broke out trade with Egypt would be
interrupted, so Herkhuf tells us he succeeded in bringing about
peace. The chief of Iam was so grateful that he gave Herkhuf a
strong escort of his own warriors to deter any attempts by the
people of Sethu and Wawat, through whose territory the returning
caravan had to pass, to attack it.

'When the chief of Arthet', the inscription says, 'and Sethu and
Wawat saw how strong and numerous was the troop of Iam which
descended with me to the court and the soldiers had been sent

with me, then this chief brought and gave to me bulls and small cattle, and conducted me to the roads of the highlands of Arthet, because I was more excellent, vigilant . . . than any Count, Companion or Caravan-Conductor who had ever been sent to Iam before.'[1]

So the modest Caravan-Conductor 'descends' to Egypt in triumph, bringing with him '300 asses laden with incense, ebony, grain, panthers, ivory, throwing-sticks, and every good product'.

He makes it sound fairly easy, but it was not. Again and again the inscriptions refer to deaths in that far-off land. Sabni's father was killed. Another Caravan-Conductor, Enenkhet, was killed by the 'Sand-dwellers', Bedouin tribesmen living near the Red Sea coast, where Enenkhet, 'Commander of the Sailors', was building a ship to sail to Punt, the 'land of perfumes' from which the Egyptians obtained much of the incense used in temple ceremonies. We know about this tragedy from another tomb, that of one Pepinakht, who thus describes it;

'Now the Majesty of my Lord sent me to the country of the Asiatics, to bring for him for Sole Companion, Commander of the Sailors, the Caravan-Conductor Enenkhet, who was building a ship there for Punt when the Asiatics belonging to the Sand-dwellers slew him, together with a troop of the army which was with him . . . and I slew people among them, I and the troop of the army which was with me.' Pepi-nakht also tell us how the king sent him to 'hack up Arthet and Wawat', whose inhabitants had again been giving trouble. It was a tough life, but rewarding if one survived.

Just *how* tough was only evident when, some years ago, archaeologists discovered and began to investigate a series of enormous castles built along the upper reaches of the Nile. I use the word castle deliberately, because the only structures with which these Ancient Egyptian fortresses can be compared are the medieval castles such as Kenilworth, Warwick and Carcasonne. There is a chain of them stretching from Buhen in the north to the twin forts of Semna and Kumma at the most southerly point of the Second Cataract. (This 'cataract', by the way, which the Egyptians call *'Batn-el-Hagar'* – 'Belly of Stones' – must not be thought of as a single waterfall. It is a 100-mile stretch of racing river, sometimes smooth and deep, but with a current so swift that only a skilful canoeist could survive in it, and often breaking into fiercely foaming rapids dashing between granite boulders.)

Along the high banks of this ravine, or on the islands which break the stream, the Ancient Egyptians, between 5,000 and 4,000 years ago, built their chain of fortresses, so sited that each could communicate with the other, probably using smoke-signals by day and beacon-fires by night. There is no other system of fortification of such age anywhere in the world, and, alas, every one of them is doomed to be destroyed when the new High Dam is completed to the south of Assouan. They cannot be moved to a safer place, partly because of their colossal size, but mainly because they are built, not of stone, but mud-brick. The Egyptian military architects used this material because it was cheap and readily available. There was little point in using stone anyway, when the most powerful weapons likely to be used against the defenders were spears and arrows. And it would take quite a time for the most determined attacker to break through walls twenty feet thick.

One glance at any of these castles, such as Buhen (Plate 12) will prove that the enemies which the Egyptians had to control were more formidable than mere groups of yelling savages. Like the castles of the European Middle Ages they were built to withstand a skilful and resourceful enemy. And like the medieval castles of the thirteenth century AD these, dating from the twentieth century BC, had a deep protective ditch surrounding the outside; and, inside, a series of mighty walls, in some cases 15 to 20 feet thick and over 30 feet high, one inside the other so that if one wall was breached the defenders could retire behind the next. They had projecting towers or bastions pierced with arrow-slits so placed as to give covering fire both in front of and alongside the wall. On the tops of the wall were sentry-walks protected by battlements. And the main entrance was usually of formidable size and strength, sometimes approached by a drawbridge.

Of these castles, Buhen, which lies at the north of the chain and was probably the headquarters of the whole defensive system, is the easiest to study in detail, since it has not only been excavated but carefully measured and recorded by Professor Emery, to whom I am indebted for much of this information, and his beautiful photographs and plans. Before long – perhaps before these words appear in print – Buhen will have been washed away by the flood water piling up behind the new High Dam, but as long as Emery's descriptions and plans survive we can know what an Egyptian frontier fortress of the Twelfth Dynasty looked like.

First turn to Plate 13 and look at Emery's reconstruction of the great West Gate of the castle. The gateway resembles the barbican of a medieval castle, and was originally approached by a drawbridge over the protecting ditch in front. Through this gateway any attacking troops would have to force their way, while the defending Egyptians poured down fire at them from the battlements. The original height of this towered gateway was over 40 feet, and the walls on each were over 30 feet in height, and nearly 20 feet thick. Now look at the plan and elevations of the castle in Plate 14. The top section shows how the defences appear from above, with the protective scarp and counterscarp (i.e. a deep straight-sided ditch to hinder the attackers, who would have first to descend the scarp and then climb the counterscarp under fire). The horseshoe-shaped bulges in the outer wall represent projecting towers with arrow-slits from which the Egyptians could fire in front and on each side, while remaining secure themselves. And beyond that was a second wall, with projecting square towers.

Professor Emery, who excavated this castle and described it in detail in his book *Egypt in Nubia* gives us a grim idea of what it must have been like to storm such a citadel.

Both the parapet and the round bastions, which have rows of loopholes arranged in groups of three, centre on a single shooting embrasure from which the defending archers could direct their arrows from three different angles downwards on to the attackers in the ditch, and level on to targets coming over the counterscarp. Some conception of the immense strength of these defences is apparent, when, standing at the bottom of the ditch, we realize that an attacking force must first storm the glacis, destroying any outposts concealed in the covered way, while under fire from sling shots and arrows from the main wall above. They would then have to descend the steep counterscarp to the bottom of the ditch, under an intense cross-fire from the loopholed ramparts and bastions, behind which the defenders would be completely concealed. Should they survive this ordeal, they would then have to storm the scarp and rampart above it, only to find themselves in a narrow corridor at the foot of the main walls, from the top of which would come a shower of stones and other missiles. . . . Nevertheless, we know that these apparently impregnable defences were breached and the fortress captured by the forces of Kush at the end of the Middle Kingdom. But looking at them even in their present ruined state we cannot help wondering if some form of treachery was not responsible for their capture.[2]

And this was only one of more than a score of fortresses stretching to the south along the tumultuous length of the Second Cataract, the 'Belly of Stones'. Some years ago an intrepid French explorer, in a canoe, made the passage of the rapids, and saw these castles as the Egyptians saw them when such men as Herkhuf and Pepi-nakht and Sabni saw some 4,600 years ago as they struggled up the ravine with their hundreds of pack-animals and troops. Or they may have avoided the rapids and taken to the desert road above; but always they knew that these fortresses (though smaller in their day, of course) were there to offer them some protection.

On the other hand, would the Ancient Egyptians have built and garrisoned these enormous fortresses *only* to protect their trading caravans? It seems to me unlikely. Surely they were intended mainly for a much more essential purpose; to protect the southern frontier of Egypt from invasion. And since one does not build on such a scale to repel attacks by half-savage tribes, the threat to Egypt, especially during the Middle and New Kingdoms, must have come from formidable and well-organized forces, at least at times. From these bases strong bodies of soldiers, sometimes in scouting patrols, at other times, if danger threatened, in battalions, would go out to meet enemies who would test their fighting skill to the limit. That was how the young men of Egypt got their experience of soldiering in the Twelfth Dynasty.

---

[1] Gardiner, A. H., *Egypt of the Pharaohs*, Clarendon Press, Oxford, 1961
[2] Emery, W. B., *Egypt in Nubia*, Hutchinson, 1965

4 Defeat and Revenge

In about 1700 BC, that is, about ninety years after the end of the powerful Twelfth Dynasty which built or rebuilt the great Nubian castles, a catastrophe struck Egypt such as the Nile Valley had never known since Hor-Aha unified the Two Lands some 1500 years earlier. This event, which the Jewish historian Josephus called the Invasion of the *Hyksos* or 'Shepherd Kings', remained a bitter and enduring memory in Egyptian hearts for as long as Egyptian civilization lasted. Perhaps to other peoples, more accustomed to invasion and occupation by foreigners, such a humiliation would have not been remembered long. But to the Egyptians it was an outrage, potent and unforgivable; so much so that they determined, when after a century and a half they threw the invaders out, that it should never happen again.

But first we must consider what the Egyptian Army was like when the invasion took place, and how it happened that a people who for fifteen centuries had been the undisputed masters of their territory lost it – or a large part of it – to mere Asiatic nomads, the very 'Sand-crossers' who had befriended Sinuhe; pastoralists and cattle-thieves, people living in tents whom the Egyptians sometimes permitted to settle in the Delta area. They were Semitic tribesmen – that is, they belonged to a race which includes the Arabs and the Jews; and some Egyptologists believe that among them were people whose descendants were the Hebrews of the Old Testament. But it must be emphasized that this event took place long before the days of Moses and the Exodus, and even longer before the founding of the kingdoms of Israel and Judea.

During the peak period of the Middle Kingdom, the Twelfth Dynasty (2000–1790 BC), the Pharaohs had won back some of the power which the monarchs of the Old Kingdom – Khufu, Chephren, Mycerinus – had enjoyed. But the nomarchs remained powerful and at times the Pharaohs had to rule through these provincial governors who were empowered to raise their own armies for their own and the King's service.

The most outstanding Pharaoh of the Twelfth Dynasty was the great Senusret III, who was almost certainly responsible for building or rebuilding the castles along the Second Cataract. Several times he had advanced through Nubia to the south at the head of his troops. The principal enemy was 'the land of Kush', the exact whereabouts of which are not certain, but it probably lay in the southern Sudan. It was probably against this formidable Kushite power that the fortresses were raised, for while the Egyptians eagerly exploited the resources of the south, especially its gold ('I visited the Mine-land as a youth', writes an official named Sihathor, 'and I forced the chiefs to wash gold'), the southerners would also be anxious to push northwards towards the more fertile part of the Nile Valley.

Senusret commanded a standing army of free-born men consisting of the 'shock-troops', the 'recruits' (probably conscripted Egyptians) and colonial troops levied from the colonies of Nubia and Libya. There was also a royal bodyguard corresponding to the Household Troops of the modern British Royal Family; these were known as 'Retainers who follow His Majesty' organized in companies of 100 men. Their officers would be drawn from important families. And in addition to all these there were soldiers recruited by the nomarchs for the Pharaoh's service.

All these soldiers were infantrymen. Cavalry and chariots had yet to be introduced to Egypt, though the skeleton of a horse was found at Buhen dating from the time of the Twelfth Dynasty – to the astonishment of archaeologists who had believed that this animal was unknown in Egypt until the time of the Hyksos invasion. The best way to understand what these troops looked like is to study some of the fascinating wooden models which were found buried in Twelfth Dynasty tombs. These, by the way, were not children's toys, though they look like them. To the Ancient Egyptians a model had magical properties. So that if you had been an officer in command of troops in your lifetime you would wish to have troops in the life to come. To kill and bury real soldiers in your tomb would be considered barbarous, though foreigners did it. But you, as an Ancient Egyptian, would be far too civilized for that sort of thing. You would know that by a process of magic the model soldiers would, in the after-life, become real live ones. But, of course, the models had to be absolutely accurate and to scale.

Look at the troops depicted in Plates 15, 16 and 17. The top picture shows a company of Egyptian infantry on the march, each stepping forward smartly 'by the left' – as in a modern army – and each man carrying in his right hand a spear and on his left arm a decorated shield of bull-hide held close to the body. They wear no helmets or body-armour, probably because the intense heat would make it uncomfortable and hinder movement. But it is noteworthy that the men wear their hair long, while civilians wore theirs short; this may have been done to give some protection to the head.

The second plate shows a company of Nubian archers, distinguishable by their darker skin. Each carries a bow and arrows at the ready, no shields, so as to be unencumbered in action, and no protective armour. These were the men who gave the Pharaoh his victories; and these would man the great forts, about 3,000 men to a fort in some cases. What is worth noticing is the smart bearing, the precision of their marching and their neat formation, all indicating a high standard of training and discipline. The models date from about 1900 BC. Incidentally why, I wonder, do marching armies always step off on the left foot? Could it be that this made the right shoulder and arm swing back, ready to make a spear or sword-thrust? The Roman legionaries also marched 'by the left', and so did all armies down to the present day.

In addition to these land troops there were, of course, the sailors of the Pharaoh's powerful navy, and marines. Among the specialized arms were axemen and slingers, beside spearmen and archers.

Ranks were well defined. The private soldier was known simply as 'a member of the army'. Discipline could be fierce and cruel. A scribe advises his pupil not to consider becoming a soldier for –

Just think of how the soldier is treated. While still a child he is shut up in the barracks. During his training he is always being knocked about. If he makes the least mistake he is beaten, a burning blow on his body, another on his eye, perhaps his head is laid open with a wound. He is battered and bruised with flogging. On the march he has to carry bread and water like the load of an ass; the joints of his back are bowed; they hang heavy loads round his neck like that of an ass. . . .

The writer of this document is clearly prejudiced, preferring the quiet life of a scribe or clerk, who pays no taxes is exempt from military service. But it is clear that he knows what pack-drill is!

As for the officers, they bore various titles, from *General, Commander of the Shock-troops, Commander of Recruits,* to *Instructor of Retainers* and *Army Scribe.* The latter, obviously, did the paper-work inseparable from any organized military force, and was responsible for stores, rationing, issuing of equipment and payment of troops. In a modern army the nearest equivalent would be the adjutant and the quartermaster-sergeant and his staff. Perhaps the best way to show you the way in which an officer secured promotion is to quote from an interesting record of the Twelfth Dynasty from the tomb of one Sebekkhu, a soldier who served under the great Senusret III. He began his career as a 'warrior of the Bodyguard' with a squad of six men. Later he rose to the rank of 'Retainer to the Ruler', commanding sixty men. Holding this not very exalted rank he took part in the Pharaoh's campaigns in Nubia, together with six other 'Instructors of Retainers', young officers of high birth with whom he probably went to school.

In a long inscription the Pharaoh himself describes how, in Year 16, the third month of the second season, he advanced from the southern boundary of his kingdom as far as a place called Heh. Senusret III boasts that 'I made my boundary beyond that of my fathers. I have increased that which was bequeathed to me.' Again and again the Pharaohs tried to outdo what their

ancestors had done. The King also boasts of his wisdom in
military matters. He knows when to strike and when to avoid
combat . . . 'attacking him who attacks . . . since, if one is
silent after attack, it strengthens the heart of the enemy. Valiance
is eagerness, cowardice is to slink back', he tells us, adding 'he is
truly a coward who is repelled upon his border'.

And just as he, Senusret, the mighty warrior, had extended his
frontier further south than his ancestors had done, so he, in his
inscription, encourages those who follow him to guard his conquests.

'Now, as for every son of mine who shall maintain this boundary
which My Majesty has made, he is my son, he is born to My
Majesty, the likeness of a son who is the champion of his father,
who maintains the boundary of him that begat him.'[1]

And here is part of the description by the young officer
Sebekkhu, who served under Senusret III, of his successive
promotions from 'Commander of Six' to 'Commander of the
Retainers'; from his stone inscription at Abydos in Egypt. After
the usual salutations to the monarch 'The Majesty of the King of
Upper and Lower Egypt, Senusret III, triumphant', who 'caused
that I should render service as a warrior', the officer continues:
'Then I was made ready at his side, and His Majesty cause that I
be appointed Retainer of the Ruler.'

'Ruler', of course, is another name for 'King' or 'Pharaoh' and a
'Retainer' was an officer in command of sixty men, whom
Sebekkhu apparently furnished himself, as, in the European
Middle Ages, a feudal lord was obliged to provide a certain
number of armed men to serve his King. Later he was promoted
to 'Instructor of the Retainers' with 100 men under his command,
after he had distinguished himself in military service. Another
officer who served under this Pharaoh's ancestor, Senusret I, tells
us that he 'followed my Lord [the Pharaoh] when he sailed southward to overthrow his enemies among the barbarians. I sailed
southward, as the son of a Count [a high nobleman], wearer of
the royal seal, and commander in chief of the Oryx-nome [one of
the provinces]'. His memorial informs us how he 'passed the land
of Kush, sailing southward', advancing 'to the boundary of the

land. . . . Then His Majesty returned in safety, having over-thrown his enemies in Kush the vile. I returned, following him with ready face. There was no loss among my soldiers.'[2]

While so powerful a Pharaoh as Senusret ruled all was well. But a time came when a succession of relatively weak monarchs allowed the power of Egypt to decline. This usually happened at times when there was no threat from the frontiers which would brace the whole nation to a united effort. The Ancient Egyptians, living comfortably in their rich, sheltered valley, were not naturally warlike, and in times of peace they usually tended to take things easily.

The Thirteenth Dynasty (1790–1700 BC) marked such a period of decay; it, together with the Fourteenth, Fifteenth and Sixteenth Dynasties (as recorded by Egyptian chroniclers of a much later date), contains the names of so many short-lived Pharaohs that it is quite impossible that they could have reigned one after the other. The solution to this problem seems to be this; that for some reason not fully understood, Egypt's unity was lost for nearly 150 years. During this time, which Egyptologists call the Second Inter-mediate Period, the country was split up, many rival Pharaohs reigning at the same time, usually for only a year or two and some-times for merely a few months. We cannot be certain how and why this happened, although a similar catastrophe befell Egypt after the collapse of the Old Kingdom in about 2270 BC (beginning of the First Intermediate Period). As Sir Alan Gardiner comments: 'Both begin with a chaotic series of insignificant native rulers; in both, intruders from Palestine cast their shadow over the Delta . . . and in both relief comes at last from a hardy race of Theban princes, who after quelling internal dissension expel the foreigner and usher in a new epoch of immense power and prosperity.'[3]

Egypt could only survive as a nation under the strong hand of a Pharaoh sufficiently powerful to command the resources of the entire land. If that controlling hand weakened, local rulers – the nomarchs – asserted themselves, governing independently of any central authority. Thus Egypt returned to an almost tribal state, as it was in predynastic days before the coming of Hor-Aha the 'Fighting Hawk'. Perhaps this did not matter much to the average

Egyptian peasant, provided he had enough to eat. He had been used to obeying his local lord, and if his lord chose to call himself the Pharaoh that would hardly worry him. But when, taking advantage of the unsettled state of Egypt, Asiatic invaders from Palestine entered Egypt and set themselves up as kings, even adopting Pharaonic titles and customs, that was very different. The Egyptians, like most peoples, resented being governed by foreigners.

The Jewish historian Josephus claims to quote the words of an Egyptian chronicler, Manetho, in describing this period of foreign rule. According to this chronicler, 'for what cause I know not, a blast of God smote us; and unexpectedly from the regions of the East invaders of an obscure race marched in confidence of victory against our land'.[4] These intruders, marching down on Egypt from what are known as the lands of Israel and Syria, seized the country after hardly striking a blow, suggesting that they chose a time when Egypt was weakened by internal struggles. Manetho says that they 'treated the natives with cruelty, massacring some and leading others, with their wives and children, into slavery'. Then they appointed one of their leaders as King, ruling from the Ancient Egyptian capital of Memphis. He also founded another city 'very favourably situated' east of the Delta, called Avaris.

Josephus calls these invaders the *Hyksos,* and suggests that the meaning of this word signifies 'captive-shepherds', the Egyptian syllable *hyk* meaning 'Shepherd'. Josephus said this because he wanted his readers to believe that this invasion of Egypt by Semitic tribesmen in about 1600 BC or earlier was the Biblical sojourn of the Jews in Egypt, followed by the Exodus in which Moses led them out again. It is a tempting theory, especially as one of these Hyksos Pharaohs was named Jacob-her and it has been suggested that this was the patriarch Jacob. However, one must be careful, because there is nothing to support this theory except the Biblical tradition, which could well refer to a much later infiltration of Hebrews into Egypt. And as for the word Hyksos, Gardiner, perhaps the world's greatest master of the Ancient Egyptian language, points out that 'it undoubtedly derives from the expression *hik-khase,* "chieftain of a foreign hill-country" which simply meant a Bedouin *sheikh* – the kind of nomad chieftain who befriended Sinuhe when he escaped from Egypt across the Sinai desert. Jews and Arabs alike are both Semites, and while it is more than likely that the Hyksos included some of the ancestors of the Biblical Hebrews, at that time there was no Jewish nation established in Palestine, and the Jews would be merely one of a large number of Bedouin tribesmen who wandered across the desert with their flocks and herds, from oasis to oasis. The fertile Delta – the northernmost part of Egypt and nearest to Asia – would always have attracted them and if, having settled there (with the permission of the Pharaohs), they found that Egypt was weak and divided among many petty kings, the temptation to take over at least the Delta region would be strong.

Certainly we can be sure that there were a number of Hyksos kings, bearing names like 'Anat-her' and 'Yakob-her', 'Apachnan' and 'Aweserre Apopi'. It is doubtful, however, if their rule extended much further south than the Delta, although they appear to have drawn tribute from Middle and Upper Egypt.

Even so, even allowing for the fact that Egypt was not ruled by one strong king, and that that gave the invaders their opportunity, it seems strange that the highly civilized Egyptians could not resist a disorderly swarm of Asiatic nomads who would have been quite incapable of building great fortresses such as those erected at the will of Senusret III, and whose armed forces are hardly likely to have equalled in discipline the smartly-turned-out infantrymen of the Twelfth Dynasty who had defeated the 'vile Kush'. How, then, did this defeat occur? Why did it occur?

Josephus, Manetho, Eusebius and other historians do not give us a clue. But the archaeologist, studying tomb and temple inscriptions, and digging in Palestine, has provided a possible answer. The Hyksos, whoever they were, had a 'blitz-weapon – the horse-drawn chariot which they had copied from the horse-rearing Mitanni of northern Mesopotamia, the people who lived within the 'Great Bend' of the Euphrates. And the Mitanni in turn got the horse from Persia, together with the art of riding it. Generally speaking the peoples of western Asia, including the Hyksos – whoever they were – were much more alert to new inventions than the Egyptians in their isolated, well-protected valley. Not only the horse but the wheel was unknown to the people who built the Great Pyramid. And though a few specimens of the horse penetrated Egypt as far back as the Twelfth Dynasty (c. 1900 BC) there is no evidence that this animal, or the swift war-chariot, were familiar in Egypt before about 1600 BC.

In the mid-twentieth century, when the horse-drawn vehicle has long been a picturesque, old-fashioned object, rarely seen, it may be difficult to see it as a revolutionary weapon as it was, not only in the hands of the Hyksos but in those of the Myceneans who invaded Greece round about this same time. Perhaps it is best to compare it with the impact made by the motor vehicle in the First World War of 1914–18. The armoured car, the truck, the tank, enabled armies to move more swiftly, although the full effect of this increased mobility was not demonstrated until the Second World War and the German *blitzkrieg* or 'lightning war' on France.

Until the coming of the Hyksos with their war-chariots and baggage-wagons the fastest pace an Egyptian army could make was the speed of its foot-slogging infantry. Suddenly the Egyptians found themselves facing an enemy which could move at the speed of a galloping horse. The Hyksos, hurtling upon them in a cloud of dust, could throw their spears and then gallop swiftly out of range, only to wheel and return again from an unexpected quarter. The effect of these manoeuvres on foot-soldiers, most of whom had probably never seen a horse, let alone a chariot, may be imagined.

Incidentally, you may wonder why the Hyksos used chariots at all; why did they not mount their horses and form cavalry units which would have been even swifter? The answer seems to be that the light horses of this period were too weak in the back to carry riders for any distance, though occasionally we see models of men riding horses. But, yoked in pairs or even fours, they could pull the lightweight chariots at speed, each chariot carrying a driver and a spearman or archer. While your companion drove the chariot you could concentrate on firing arrows or hurling spears at the enemy.

Under the fury of such attacks the Egyptian infantry-soldiers collapsed, their spirits broken, and the triumphant Hyksos were able to take over the Delta and even penetrate some distance southward. But they do not appear to have exercised direct control over Middle and Upper Egypt (i.e. southward of Memphis). Nevertheless, there they were, comfortably settled in the richest part of Egypt, with their kings at Avaris (which is probably modern Tanis). To the south, at Thebes, some 600 miles away, a family of local Theban princes set themselves up as Pharaohs, but their pretensions were not taken seriously by the Hyksos lords of Avaris, one of whom wrote scornfully to the lord of Thebes, complaining that the noise of the hippopotami at the Pharaoh's capital kept him awake at night!

The name of the Egyptian Pharaoh was Sekenre (Sek-en-*ray*), who reigned near the end of the Seventeenth Dynasty, when the Hyksos usurpers were ruling from Avaris. We cannot be certain from documentary evidence that Sekenre made war on the Hyksos; but by a miraculous chance his corpse has survived and is now on view in the archaeological museum in Cairo. His skull bears the marks of hideous wounds, and his face is twisted in the agony of violent death. It is more than likely that he met his death whilst leading his troops against the Hyksos, because at this time the Egyptians had begun to revolt against foreign domination. We know that Sekenre's successors of the Eighteenth Dynasty (1555–1350 BC) challenged the invaders and in a series of battles drove them beyond the frontiers of Egypt. One would like to think that Sekenre was the first 'fighting Pharaoh' of the New Kingdom (1555–712 BC). But there is no proof; he could well have been assassinated by agents of the Hyksos king.

There can be little doubt that when the Eighteenth Dynasty dawned there was nothing like a modern movement of national liberation arising almost spontaneously from the spirits of an oppressed people. The movement came from the princes of Thebes, who, until then, had been little more than nomarchs, although they called themselves Pharaohs. But during the bitter years which followed the collapse of the Old Kingdom in about

2270 BC the ancestors of these Theban princes had taken the lead in restoring order throughout the land; perhaps the memory of those glorious days had been kept alive in Thebes. But for whatever reason, under the leadership of vigorous and warlike rulers, the Egyptians began to take the offensive against the intruding Asiatics.

As recently as 1954 an Egyptian archaeologist named Labib Habachi made a wonderful discovery; at Karnak he unearthed a 'victory stela' in which the Theban king Kamose (successor to Sekenre) commemorates incidents in his successful struggle with the Hyksos king Aweserre Apopi. This record is so vivid that it reads like a series of war-dispatches dictated by Kamose (pronounced Ka-*mo*-zay) in the heat of action. He appears to have begun with a combined naval and military operation directed from his river-fleet as they sailed downstream, mopping up the strongholds of the Hyksos vassal-chiefs.

I fared downstream in might to overthrow the Asiatics by the command of Amun (god of Thebes) the just of counsels; my brave army in front of me like a breath of fire, the troops of Medju (Nubians) aloft upon our cabins to spy out the Setyu and destroy their places. East and West were in possession of their fat and the army was supplied with things everywhere.[5]

And in a later passage occur these words;

I spent the night in my ship, my heart happy. When the earth became light, I was upon him as it were a hawk. The time of perfuming the mouth came, and I overthrew him, I razed his wall, I slew his people and I caused his wife to go to the river-bank. My soldiers were like lions with their prey, with serfs, cattle, milk, fat, and honey, dividing up their possessions.

At this stage of the operations Kamose was making war on his own countrymen, as is clear from another passage; but these Egyptians on whom he was making war had, according to the royal chronicler, betrayed their country by supporting the Asiatic rulers against their fellow Egyptians. Therefore they deserved no pity, and received none.

I razed their towns and burned their places, they being made into red ruins forever on account of the damage which they did within this Egypt, and they had made themselves serve the Asiatics and had forsaken Egypt their mistress.

And Kamose's burning hatred of the invaders comes out clearly when he says:

Your heart is undone, base Asiatic, who used to say 'I am lord, and there is none equal to me from Khmun and Pi-Hathor down to Avaris . . .'

Another passage from this exciting document describes how Kamose captured a messenger travelling between Avaris and the capital of the King of Kush in the far south. In the envoy's 'diplomatic bag' was a letter from Aweserre, the Hyksos king, to the Kushite monarch. It read;

Aweserre, the son of Re, Apopi greet my son the chieftain of Kush. Why have you arisen as chieftain without letting me know; Have you (not) beheld what Egypt has done against me, and the chieftain who is in it, Kamose the Mighty, ousting me from my soil and I have not reached him – after the manner of all that he has done against you, he choosing the two lands to devastate them, my land and yours, and he has destroyed them. Come, fare north at once, do not be timid. See, he is here with me. . . . I will not let him go until you have arrived. Then we will divide the towns of this Egypt between us.[6]

At the end of the stela Kamose tells how he returned to Thebes in triumph, where the population, according to his account, greeted him as a conqueror. But he died before he could complete the task of driving the hated enemy from Egyptian soil. That honour was left to his successor Ahmose (Ah-*mo*-say), founder of the glorious Eighteenth Dynasty and one of a long line of fighting Pharaohs.

[1] Emery, W. B., *Egypt in Nubia*, Hutchinson, 1965
[2] Breasted, J. H., *Ancient Records of Egypt*, Chicago University Press; 1906
[3] Gardiner, A. H., *Egypt of the Pharaohs*, Clarendon Press, Oxford, 1961
[4] Gardiner, A. H., op. cit.
[5] Gardiner, A. H., op. cit.
[6] Gardiner, A. H., op. cit.

5 The Fighting Tuthmosids

The founding of the Eighteenth Dynasty marked the beginning of a new and glorious epoch in Egypt's history, comparable with the unification of the Two Lands by Hor-Aha more than 1,500 years earlier. In some ways it was even more remarkable than that event, because whereas Hor-Aha (or Menes) created a united nation, the Pharaoh Ahmose (Ah-*mo*-say) and his successors of the Eighteenth Dynasty founded an empire. During their vigorous reigns, beginning in about 1555 BC, the hated Hyksos invaders were first flung out of Egypt and then pursued relentlessly into and beyond their homelands, defeated and routed by the same weapon which they themselves had introduced to Egypt – the horse-drawn chariot. From this period onwards the Egyptian Army changed. Though there were still bowmen and spearmen as in the Middle Kingdom, there were also charioteers. And for a time these intrepid warriors, led by Pharaohs who were skilful fighting generals and not only kings, became the most terrifying mobile fighting force in the world.

There can be no doubt that when Kamose's successor Ahmose, first Pharaoh of the Eighteenth Dynasty, came to the throne, Egypt was still in danger. Kamose, and his predecessor Sekenre, had won some victories, but, in the south, the great castles strung along the Second Cataract were attacked and taken by an unknown enemy, almost certainly the 'vile Kush'. Even Buhen, most powerful of all, and headquarters of the Viceroy of Nubia, shows the tell-tale marks of fire and sacking. From the letter which Kamose had intercepted it is clear that the Hyksos king Apopi, whose capital was at Avaris in the Delta, regarded the King of Kush as his ally. Thus Egypt was subjected to a 'pincer movement' from the north and the south.

The founders of the Eighteenth Dynasty were princes of Thebes, until then a mere nome or province, although certain Pharaohs of the Thirteenth Dynasty had reigned from there. There were fifteen kings of the Eighteenth Dynasty, whose reigns are well attested. Of these, eight were remarkable fighting-men and four bore the name Tuthmosis (in some books spelt Thothmes or Thuthmose), collectively known as the Tuthmosids. Throughout the entire history of Ancient Egypt there has never been such a succession of brave, resolute and skilful generals, one of whom, Tuthmosis III, has been described as 'the Napoleon of Ancient Egypt'.

But it is necessary to sound a note of caution here. One must not take too seriously the statement that the Hyksos kings were cruel tyrants and that 'they burned our cities ruthlessly, razed to the ground the temples of the gods, and treated all the natives with cruel hostility, massacring some and leading into slavery the wives and children of others'. As Sir Alan Gardiner points out, similar statements, almost word-for-word, were made whenever Egypt was threatened by attack from foreigners. It was, he tells us, 'a type of literary fiction which became an established convention of Egyptian historical writing; a period of desolation and anarchy is painted in exaggeratedly lurid colours, usually for the glorification of a monarch to whom the salvation of the country is ascribed'.[1]

Propaganda is not a new method of influencing people's minds, but has a history going back thousands of years. The fact seems to be that the Hyksos never ruled the area south of the Delta, though it appears that they had brought some of the southern nomarchs on to their side, and secured the help of the kings of Kush. But the Ancient Egyptians, like the modern successors, hated foreign rule, however mild, and were eager to follow the leadership of the Eighteenth Dynasty Pharaohs, who offered them liberty and later the opportunity of looting and punishing the foreigners in their own territory.

And there was another aspect of this struggle which must be remembered, the religious aspect. The Egyptians, from those very early times before Hor-Aha united the Two Lands, had worshipped their own native gods, of whom there were many. Each nome (originally a tribal area) had its own hierarchy of gods and goddesses. The chief god of Thebes, for instance, was Amun, originally a minor deity with the head of a ram. When the princes of Thebes became powerful their god also became more important than most of the other gods, and eventually he was united with the god of the Memphite nome, the sun-god Re, under the title Amun-Re. Propaganda entered into this, too. It pleased the Egyptian rulers of Thebes to lay all their victories at the feet of Amun-Re, whose priests urged the Pharaoh to conquer in his name. This does not mean that the deities worshipped in the other nomes became out of date; they remained important, but such gods as Ptah of Memphis, Khnum, Horus and Osiris, to name only a few, became subordinate to Amun-Re, just as the nomes in which these gods and goddesses were worshipped became subject to the ruling dynasty of Thebes.

Most of what we know concerning the victories of the Eighteenth Dynasty Pharaohs comes from inscriptions in the temples of the gods; that is, accounts of royal triumphs, suitably recorded in rather pompous language. But there are other sources of information which in certain ways are more realistic and convincing. Egyptologists have discovered, in various places, inscriptions in the tombs of minor servants of the king; soldiers who had fought beside him on the battlefield and been rewarded by him with 'the Gold of praise'. These straightforward accounts of warfare under the monarchs of the New Kingdom are usually more realistic than the somewhat high-flown accounts left by the Pharaohs themselves (or their royal scribes).

At a place called El Kab there are the ruined tombs of two such officers, both named Ahmose, like the king who began the Eighteenth Dynasty. But as far as we know they were not of royal blood; probably they took the royal name for the reason that some of us name our children Elizabeth or Charles. The elder Ahmose of El Kab served under several Pharaohs, the first being the valiant Ahmose whose namesake he was. He was quite an old warrior when he died, and has much to tell us. Here he is describing an attack on the Hyksos king's capital at Avaris in the far north of Egypt, a long way from Thebes, after first telling us proudly that his father Ebana had fought under Sekenre.

'I spent my youth in the city of Nekheb, my father being an officer of the King . . . Sekenre, triumphant. . . . Then I served as an officer in my father's place, in the ship called "The Offering". This was in the time of King Ahmose I, triumphant, while I was still young, not having taken a wife, and while I was still sleeping in a hammock' (as an ordinary sailor, that is).

But Ahmose (the sailor) prospered, took himself a wife and started a family. Some time later he was, in his own words, 'transferred to the Northern Fleet because of my valour'. But he also served the King as a foot soldier 'on my two feet when he rode abroad in his chariot'. Probably, among the Ancient Egyptians, there was not the clear distinction which exists today between sailors and soldiers (except for the Marines).

When the Pharaoh besieged the Hyksos city of Avaris, Ahmose 'showed valour on foot before His Majesty; then I was appointed to the ship [called] "Shining-in-Memphis" '. This was evidently a combined naval and land battle where the Pharaoh used his naval force to approach the Delta city, which was probably surrounded by canals, since Ahmose says that he 'fought in the canal against Pezedku of Avaris. There I fought hand-to-hand. I brought away a hand' (cut off as a trophy from a slain foe) 'and it was reported to the royal herald.' And our hero received a high military distinction, 'the gold of valour', from the Pharaoh himself.

Again he fights at Avaris in a third battle in which 'I fought hand-to-hand there; I brought away another hand'. And again he received 'the gold of bravery' (or of valour) from the King. Apparently the siege of Avaris was interrupted by rebellion in the south, and yet again Ahmose distinguished himself, bringing away 'a living captive', no doubt someone of high importance, for once again his reward was 'gold in double measure'.[2]

Eventually the Pharaoh Ahmose captured Avaris, with his namesake taking captive 'one man and three women, total four heads; His Majesty gave them to me for slaves'. Next the Pharaoh besieged a city called Sharuhen *for three years,* and eventually took it. This must have been a formidable fortress to which the Hyksos, having lost their capital, retreated to make their last stand. It speaks much for the persistence of the royal warrior and his followers that he was able to maintain this siege for so long until at last the citadel of Hyksos resistance collapsed.

Our friend Ahmose was there at the taking of the city, of course, and again received 'the gold of valour' from the Pharaoh for his services. No doubt it was these repeated awards, and loot taken in combat, which enabled him to pay for his impressive tomb at El Kab. A later part of the tomb inscription records a fight in Nubia, where, in the Pharaoh's absence, the 'Troglodytes' (cave-dwellers) had risen in rebellion.

> Now, after His Majesty had slain the Asiatics [i.e. the Hyksos] he ascended the river to Khenthennofer, to destroy the Nubian Troglodytes; His Majesty made great slaughter among them. Then I took captive there two living men, and took three hands [i.e. two prisoners of war and slew three foes]. One presented me with gold in double measure, besides giving me two female slaves. His Majesty sailed downstream, his heart joyous with the might of victory, for he had seized Southerners and Northerners.[3]

You may say that this is not very much to describe the military achievements of one of the mightiest of the Pharaohs, the liberator of Egypt. Alas, it is practically all we have, because though other records must have existed they have all perished, or at least not yet been found. Imagine that, 3,000 years from now, all that remained to future historians to describe the Battle of Britain was the log of one R.A.F. fighter pilot; and all that survived to tell the story of, say Corregidor, were a few scraps from the diary of one United States sailor. That, more or less, is the situation concerning the Warrior Pharaoh Ahmose of the Eighteenth Dynasty.

The other Ahmose of El Kab served not only under the Pharaoh Ahmose but under his successors Amenophis I, Tuthmosis I, Tuthmosis II, and Tuthmosis III. He simply says;

'I was with Their Majesties when they went to the North and South Country, in every place where they went, from King Ahmosis I, triumphant' . . . and then follows a list of four

Pharaohs ending with Tuthmosis III. Not surprisingly, this veteran soldier 'attained a good old age, having had a life of royal favour, having had honour under Their Majesties'.

And among the gifts he received from these various monarchs for his valour in action he mentions 'bracelets, necklaces, armlets, daggers, gold axes, silver axes, a fan and a head-dress'. It must be remembered that there was no such thing as coinage in Ancient Egypt. Payment was always made in goods, whether these took the form of golden jewellery, cattle, or grants of land. What the common soldiers received for risking their lives in the Pharaoh's cause is not stated. No doubt, if they survived, they would be lucky if they could bring back to Egypt some of the plunder of the enemy after the Pharaoh, his high officers, and the priests of Amun had taken their pick.

But many would have died in these battles, not only from enemy weapons but from disease, thirst and starvation. Again it must be remembered that many wounds which in our time could be healed by modern medicine would have proved fatal to Egyptian soldiers, especially those of ordinary rank. Physicians did accompany the armies, but in general their services would be occupied by the higher ranks of the army. In this respect, at least, the modern soldier is better off.

The Pharaoh Ahmose, after a reign of about twenty-one years, was succeeded by Amenophis I (1550–1528 BC). He seems to have been as stern a fighter as his father, and both the Ahmoses of El Kab served under him, too. Again we have to rely mainly on them for the brief information concerning their military achievements, although there are some rock-cut inscriptions at various points along the river set up by the kings themselves, recording the extent of their conquests.

Ahmose, son of Ebana tells us that he 'sailed the King Amenophis I when he ascended the river to Kush' – that is, he was in command of the royal warship when His Majesty went to chastise the Nubians of Egypt's ancient enemy, the land of Kush, sometimes known as 'Kush the vile'. Some of these southern foes were evidently cave-dwellers (troglodytes), since the inscription goes on to say that 'His Majesty captured that Nubian Troglodyte in the midst of his army. . . . I was at the head of our army; I fought incredibly; His Majesty beheld my bravery' . . . and so on, in typical Egyptian manner.

The more modest Ahmose contents himself with saying that he followed King Amenophis I, captured for him in Kush a living prisoner, and, in another campaign – this time in Libya – served the Pharaoh Amenophis I, capturing for him 'in the north of Imukekek three hands'. Again, capturing three prisoners does not sound much to brag about, but one can be almost certain that these would be especially distinguished prisoners, men of rank, valuable as hostages and perhaps as sources of ransom.

When Amenophis I died he left no son to succeed him, which was extremely unusual for a Pharaoh. Perhaps he had had sons, but they may have died young, or perhaps in the fighting which occupied such a large part of this Pharaoh's reign. When he died, in about 1528 BC Thebes had risen from a mere provincial city to become the capital of Egypt. It was not yet the splendid place which was to become a legend in later years, abounding in towering temples and deep-hewn tombs which even today, in ruin, excite the wondering imagination. But it was well on its way. Temples to Amun-Re and other Theban deities had arisen on the east bank, while opposite, beyond the broad, smooth-flowing Nile, rose the deep-fissured white limestone cliffs, a mighty backdrop to the funerary temples rising at their feet, and the richly furnished royal and noble tombs which gangs of workmen hollowed from their depths. The coffin of the great Kamose himself was discovered there in 1857, but the body crumbled to dust when exposed to the air. Among the treasures buried with it, however, was a magnificent ceremonial dagger now in Brussels.

Kamose, incidentally, may have been the short-lived brother of Ahmose; their mother, whose name was Ahhotpe, lived to a great age and her coffin and mummy were discovered and are now in the Cairo Museum. An inscription states that she rallied the soldiery of Egypt and put an end to a rebellion. This might have happened during the unsettled period between the death of Kamose and the accession of Ahmose, founder of the Eighteenth Dynasty.

What is extraordinary, considering how short-lived many
civilizations have been, is the way that of Ancient Egypt, already
more than 1,500 years old, drew new life and vigour from these
Warrior Pharaohs of Thebes, after a century and a half of foreign
domination. Even more amazing, the Egyptians were not merely
content to throw the invaders out, which they had done by the
time of Amenophis 1, but went on to found a great overseas
empire and become, for a long period, the richest and most powerful state on earth.

Successor to Amenophis 1 was the first of four Pharaohs bearing the name Tuthmosis. Ahmose, son of Ebana of El Kab, served
with him, too, as he proudly informs us in his tomb inscription.
Describing an expedition into Nubia, the old warrior says:

I sailed the King Tuthmosis 1, triumphant, when he ascended the river to
Khenthennofer, in order to cast out violence in the highlands, in order to
suppress the raiding of the hill region. I showed bravery in his presence in
the bad water, in the passage of the ship by the bend. One (i.e. the Pharaoh)
appointed me chief of the sailors.

The 'highlands' were the upland regions of the Upper Nile
where much violence had taken place. The 'bad water' means the
fierce rapids – evidently notorious to Egyptian navigators, since
the reader is supposed to know which 'bend' was meant. The
Nile bends and twists greatly in its upper reaches and the water
flows fast. Ahmose, in command of the King's flagship, had a
great responsibility which he discharged so well that the Pharaoh
honoured him by giving him a high naval command – 'chief of
the sailors'.

Here follows a break in the inscription, which begins again at
a point where Ahmose is describing the Pharaoh's anger at the
enemy's threats.

His Majesty was furious thereat, like a panther; His Majesty cast his first
lance, which remained in the body of that fallen one. This was . . . powerless
before his flaming uraeus [the royal serpent in the Pharaoh's battle-helmet],
made so in an instant of destruction; their people were brought off as living
prisoners. His Majesty sailed down-river, with all the countries in his grasp,
that wretched Nubian Troglodyte being hanged head downward at the prow
of the ship of his Majesty, and landed at Karnak.[4]

And Ahmose's inscription ends with a final description of His Majesty's campaign in Syria Palestine, the Land of Retenu, where Sinuhe had been befriended by the chieftain Ammi-Enshi some 400 years earlier.

The Pharaoh led his armies first to the district of Naharin, a name which occurs frequently in Egyptian chronicles; it was on the Euphrates. Here a bitter battle took place at which a great slaughter was made. 'Numberless were the living prisoners which His Majesty brought off from his victories. Meanwhile I was at the head of our troops, and His Majesty beheld my bravery.' Again the warrior captures an important prisoner . . . 'I brought off a chariot, its horses, and him who was upon it and took them to His Majesty', who rewarded him 'with gold in double measure'. And the writer adds that even in old age he continued to receive rich rewards.

It is all very bold and conventional, this story. But most tomb inscriptions were like this; and as for the royal stelae (inscribed stones) which the Pharaohs set up to commemorate their triumphs, these may be longer and more fulsome, but to our ears, accustomed to realistic descriptions of warfare, artificial and often boring. What we have to do is to fill the gaps with our imaginations, aided by what we can see today of the countries in which these actions took place, and what archaeologists can teach us from tomb inscriptions, carved temple relief and battle scenes, and the weapons sometimes found in tombs. Very occasionally one finds what to my mind is the most evocative of all – time-worn rock-cut inscriptions in far-off Palestine and Syria, left by a Pharaoh who passed that way more than thirty centuries ago.

captains and rulers clothed most gorgeously, horsemen riding upon horses, all of them desirable young men . . . with chariots, wagons, and wheels, and with an assembly of people. . . .[5]

---

[1] Gardiner, A. H., *Egypt of the Pharaohs,* Clarendon Press, Oxford, 1961

[2] Breasted, J. H., *Ancient Records of Egypt,* Vol. 2. Chicago University Press, 1906

[3] Breasted, J. H., op. cit.

[4] Breasted, J. H., op. cit.

[5] Breasted, J. H., op. cit.

6 The Napoleon of Ancient Egypt

. . . the good God, who smites the Nubians, lord of might, who overthrows the Asiatics. He made his boundary as far as the Horns of the Earth, and the marshes in Kebeh. . . . The Sand-dwellers bore their tribute like the impost of the South and North; His Majesty forwarded them to Thebes, for his father Amun, each year.[1]

This inscription in the tomb of an official named Ineni (ee-*nay*-nee) refers to the conquests of Tuthmosis I, under whom Ahmose of El Kab, son of Ebana, also served at Naharin and elsewhere. Ineni was not a soldier but a high servant. Among his titles were Overseer of the Granary and Chief Architect of the King's monuments. Brief though it is, this inscription tells us a great deal about the military achievements of Tuthmosis. The 'Horns of the Earth' refer to the southland beyond Wadi Halfa. The 'marshes in Kebeh' were not in Egypt but far away in northern Syria, along the banks of the Euphrates. This gives some idea of the wide-ranging extent of Tuthmosis's conquests. Naharin also, mentioned in the account by Ahmose of El Kab at the end of the preceding chapter, was in northern Syria.

At ancient Abydos, one of the most sacred sites in Egypt, there is a stone stela in the temple of Osiris in which Tuthmosis I records a speech to the priests of the temple in which he says that he extended the boundaries of Egypt 'as far as that which the sun encircles'. This extravagant claim can be best understood by remembering that to the Ancient Egyptians of this period the world consisted of their own country, plus parts of the lands south, east, west and north-east of it. They had no knowledge of even the west Mediterranean, let alone middle and northern Europe; nor could they have had any idea of the vastness of the African continent as we know it. Tuthmosis goes on to say that he 'made strong those who were in fear', i.e. his armies protected those whose lands had been threatened or overrun by invaders, and that he 'made Egypt superior of every land'.

When Tuthmosis I died he was the first Pharaoh to be buried in the Valley of the Kings' tombs. Before his reign the princes of Thebes had been buried in front of the line of cliffs, between them and the river. But behind the cliffs lay a hidden valley approached along a narrow wadi, and here the king's architect and Overseer of Works supervised the quarrymen who hewed out the first royal sepulchre in what was to become the richest mausoleum on earth. He did this, no doubt at the Pharaoh's instructions, in the hope that the royal tomb would escape robbery in later times.

'I was in charge of the excavation of the cliff-tomb of His Majesty, which was done in secret, no-one seeing, no-one hearing. I sought out the excellent things. . . . I was vigilant in seeking that which is excellent' (for the tomb). 'I made fields of clay in order to produce fine plaster for covering the inner walls of the tomb. It was a work which our ancestors had never done which I was obliged to do there, and I shall be praised for my wisdom by those who come after me, and those who will imitate what I have done. . . . '

It is typical of the simplicity of the Egyptian mind that Ineni, having taken enormous trouble to build a secret tomb for the Pharaoh, boasts about it in large hieroglyphs in his own more modest sepulchre. Or perhaps he was so vain that he believed that no one would ever find his own tomb and read the inscription inside it. But more likely that he did not see the illogicality of his action, for when an Ancient Egyptian did anything which he considered extraordinary he had to tell the world about it. As for the workmen who made the tomb, and shared the secret, there is absolutely no evidence to suggest that they were killed afterwards. This may have been because the Egyptian rulers were too humane, or because good quarrymen were scarce! So, of course, the secrets were not kept, and every tomb in the Royal Valley was wholly or partly robbed, even that of Tutankhamun. Yet by a miracle, as we shall see later, most of the royal bodies have survived down to this day.

But although Tuthmosis I had been a mighty warrior, extending Egypt's conquests far into the north and south, the task was not over. His successor, Tuthmosis II, had to fight hard both in Nubia and Syria-Palestine. An inscription at Assouan relates how, 'the rebellious barbarians, the Nubian Troglodytes among the children of the chief of the wretched Kush', had to be trounced once again. 'His majesty was furious thereat, like a panther . . .' (just like his father, as Sir Alan Gardiner comments) 'when he heard it. His Majesty said "I swear, as Re loves me, as my father, lord of gods, Amun, lord of Thebes, favours me, I will not let live anyone among their males among them".'

The rest of this boastful inscription, no doubt compiled by a scribe, describes how 'This army of His Majesty overthrew those barbarians; they did not let live anyone among their males . . . except one of those children of the chief of the wretched Kush, who was taken away as a living prisoner' (and no doubt as a hostage, to be brought up at the Egyptian Court).

A strange and intriguing situation arose at the Theban Court on the death of Tuthmosis II. It can best be illustrated by the fact that in the lists of kings and their reign dates kept by the Egyptians of later times the name Tuthmosis II is followed immediately by that of Tuthmosis III. Yet we know for a certain fact, from other sources, that Tuthmosis III, greatest of all the Warrior Pharaohs, did not rule Egypt as sole monarch until sixteen years later. In the meantime Egypt was governed by Queen Hatshepsut (sometimes spelt Hashepsowe), widow of Tuthmosis II and daughter of Tuthmosis I. She was a woman of strong, dominant character. Her nephew (who was also her stepson), Tuthmosis III, was a mere child when Tuthmosis II died, so that according to Ancient Egyptian custom she had the right to reign as regent until the boy came of age. But she so loved authority that she kept Tuthmosis from any active exercise of power until he was at least in his early twenties, long after he should by right have reigned as sole and undisputed king.

The west fortifications of the Middle Kingdom fortress at Buhen
(about 2000 B.C.)   *Walter B. Emery*

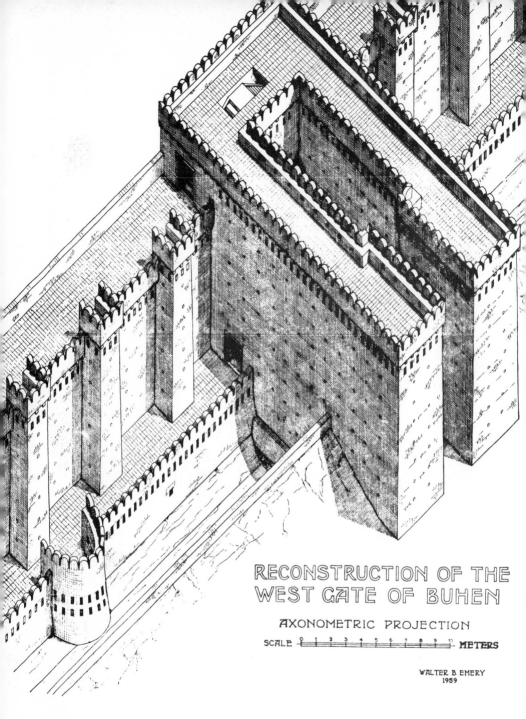

RECONSTRUCTION OF THE WEST GATE OF BUHEN

AXONOMETRIC PROJECTION

SCALE |0 1 2 3 4 5 6 7 8 9 10| METERS

WALTER B. EMERY
1959

Reconstruction of the West Gate of Buhen by Professor Emery
Walter B. Emery

Closeup of the Nubian archers. The wood models are depicted carrying bows and arrows at the ready   *Walter B. Emery*

A company of Egyptian infantry on the march. A group of wooden soldiers from a Twelfth-Dynasty tomb   *Roger Wood*

A company of Nubian archers   *Walter B. Emery*

As a result of this he hated her and her advisers, especially a certain Sen-en-mut who was her closest friend. Also she must have been very unpopular with the friends of the young king, and most likely the ordinary Egyptian also suspected and distrusted her. For the Egyptians, while they respected and admired their queens, did not want a woman ruling over them in her own right. If she was a queen by virtue of being married to the reigning Pharaoh, that was all right. But Hatshepsut's husband was dead, and though she had royal blood in her veins this did not give her the right to rule if there was a rightful male claimant to the throne. The trouble here was that the young man who became the third Tuthmosis (and the greatest) was not the son of Hatshepsut. His mother was a minor wife of her husband, Tuthmosis II, named Ese (Isis) – the Pharaohs had several wives beside the Queen, who was known as 'Chief Wife'. Because her husband Tuthmosis II was also her half-brother, Hatshepsut was also the third Tuthmosis's aunt, and she became his stepmother after the death of Ese. But Hatshepsut was also the daughter of a Pharaoh and the widow of a Pharaoh. It may have been this, as much as her love of power, which caused her to become the chief ruler of Egypt, while the boy Tuthmosis remained in the background for so long.

She was not interested in warfare. Perhaps she had enough of it, having been brought up in the warlike atmosphere of the Theban court by her military father, and then married to another military man. Yet she ruled wisely and well, building a magnificent temple at Deir el Bahri and sending an important trading mission to the Land of Perfumes (Punt). What her young stepson was doing during these long peaceful years is not known, but, in view of his brilliance as a military commander in later years, it seems highly probable that he spent them in training with the army.

Legally he was king, but his actual position is tactfully described by Ineni in his tomb;

Having ascended into heaven, he (Tuthmosis II) became united with the gods, and his son, being arisen in his place as King of the Two Lands, ruled upon the throne of his begetter, *while his sister, the god's wife Hatshepsut governed the land and the Two Lands were under her control; people worked for her, and Egypt bowed the head.*[2]

It is unlikely that the man whom Tuthmosis proved himself to be would have loafed at the Court of Hatshepsut, with Sen-en-mut and her other advisers; he would be more at home with the soldiers with whom he was to campaign for the better part of his reign; and there is a strong suggestion that when he at last came to power he did so with their aid. But equally it would be wrong to think of him necessarily as a young firebrand, itching to unseat his stepmother from the throne in order to fling Egypt into war again. Hatshepsut enjoyed sixteen years of peace, but they had been won for her by her fighting ancestors.

When she disappeared from the scene, in the sixteenth year of the joint reign, Egypt's ancient enemies were again threatening, but this time the danger did not come only from the 'vile Asiatics' whom the Pharaohs had driven from the Nile Valley, but from other, stronger powers which were arising in what are today northern Iraq and Turkey. These were the Mitanni, whose kingdom had been established along the 'Great Bend' of the Euphrates (see map) and the much more powerful Hittites of Asia Minor, whom the Egyptians called 'the abominable Kheta'. Neither of these powers threatened Egypt directly, as yet, but they were menacing the Egyptian possessions and subject states in Syria-Palestine. Having won an empire for themselves, the Pharaohs now had to defend it. They were no longer isolated in their valley, content unto themselves. They had become what we call a 'world power', although the civilized 'world' of 1500 BC was confined mainly to the east Mediterranean and the lands to the east of it comprising what geographers used to call the 'Fertile Crescent'.

This, as you will see from a glance at the map on page 4, comprised the Nile Valley, the valleys of the Tigris and Euphrates, and some of the fertile territory in between. But in south-eastern Europe other civilizations had risen; the Mycenaeans, ancestors of the classical Greeks, were strongly established in Greece and some of the Aegean islands, while on the island of Crete a rich and civilized sea-power had grown up, more advanced than Mycenae and in many ways equal to Egypt; these European civilizations, however, were too far off to be a threat to Egypt, who merely traded with them. But the Hittites, established in their mountain stronghold in Asia Minor to the far north, had already begun to penetrate into Syria, and rumbling of their slow advance was heard in far-off Thebes, passed on in the messages which the Pharaoh received from his Syrian vassals.

Not that the Hittites presented an immediate threat to the Egyptians when the young Tuthmosis III, free at last of his step-mother's control, led his armies in the Lebanon and Syria in his first Asiatic campaign. The Hittites were still far off to the north. The immediate enemy were the 'vile Asiatics' led by the King of Kadesh, a powerful, strategically placed city at the northern end of the B'ka Valley in the Lebanon, between twin ranges of mountains. The site is worth memorizing because on more than one occasion it saw much bloodshed. Any army approaching Syria from the south had to pass Kadesh to reach the plains of Syria unless it took the longer coastal route.

The army which Tuthmosis III commanded was very different from those of such Middle Kingdom Pharaohs as Senusret and Amenemhat. There were still considerable bodies of infantrymen (foot-sloggers) carrying spears, swords and shields. There were axemen, spearmen and archers, all on foot. But since the rise of the New Kingdom under Ahmose and the first two Tuthmosids there had been what amounted to a revolution in military methods. First, there was now a large regular army organized on a national basis and owing direct allegiance to the king. This army was officered by professional soldiers, not local lords who gave their services and recruited men for the duration of one war.

Secondly, the most important and effective arm was now the chariot force. The chariots were very light, very fast two-wheeled vehicles drawn by swift horses trained for battle. Each chariot carried two warriors, one to drive and the other to hurl spears or shoot from the bow. Approaching out of the sun in a cloud of desert sand, with the combined roar of their massed wheels and galloping hoofs shaking the earth, the Egyptian chariotry were terrifying to the enemy, if well led. They might be approximately compared with the armoured divisions of a modern army with their tanks, half-tracks, armoured cars and so on.

This is not an exact comparison, because in a modern army the tank is better protected, by armour, against enemy attack than the infantry soldier. Egyptian chariots were not armoured and their crews were just as vulnerable as the men who fought on foot. Their main protection lay in their speed and manoeuvrability. Perhaps a more accurate comparison would be with a modern air fighter force.

How was this new army organized and officered? At the very top stood the Pharaoh, who usually took the field himself as Commander-in-Chief except in minor campaigns. Next to him in rank was the Vizier, who in civil life might be compared with a Prime Minister, but who was also Minister for War. He was assisted by an Army Council to whom he gave orders. But when campaigning in the field the Pharaoh relied on a council of senior officers whose advice he sought, but did not always follow, as we shall see. The army was organized in divisions consisting of about 5,000 men, each with its divisional commander. These divisions usually had names, so that we read of 'the divisions of Amun, of Re, and Sutekh' – all names of gods. There were also 'second' divisions, probably reserve troops.

Each division, like that of a modern army, was a self-contained unit including both chariotry and infantry, and the divisional commanders were royal princes, except for one division which was usually led by the Pharaoh himself in his war-chariot. Such an army, of upwards of 20,000 men, must have been a splendid sight, whether on the march or deployed in battle array. Under the cloudless sky of Syria, against a background of purple mountains, the mighty host would be seen far off, the sun glinting on the massed spear-heads, on the waving banners of the regiments, and on the gold mountings of the royal and princely chariots. And a great sound would come from it, a mingling of marching feet, rumbling of chariot wheels, clatter of horses' hoofs, and the murmur of many men.

As for the sight and sound of such an army in combat, there is no more poetic description than that in the Book of Isaiah;

> Hast thou given the horse his strength?
> Hast thou clothed his neck with thunder?
> Canst thou make him afraid as a grasshopper?

The glory of his nostrils is terrible. . . .
He sayeth among the trumpets 'Ha ha'
And he smelleth the battle afar off
The thunder of the captains, and the shouting. . . .

As for the 'chain of command', the lowest grade of officer was called 'the greatest of fifty'; above him came the 'standard-bearer' commanding a regiment of 200 (in later times 250) men. Above these regimental commanders came the 'captain of a troop' and next 'the commander of a troop'. Possibly a troop commander headed a brigade of several regiments; he could also be the commandant of a fortress, in which case, above him, there would be the 'overseer of garrison troops' and 'overseer of fortresses'. But, these two latter would usually be administrators rather than active soldiers. Still higher than the 'troop commander' came the 'general' and highest of all, next to the Pharaoh himself, was the 'general-issimo'.

Of course, you must bear in mind that these names are only the nearest we can get, in English, to the meaning of the Ancient Egyptian names. The originals are shorter and crisper; for instance, a 'captain of a troop' was a *ts pdt* and his senior, a troop commander, was a *hry pdt*. Unfortunately as the vowel sounds are missing we have no idea how these names were pronounced; this, alas, is true of nearly all Ancient Egyptian names. But what is fascinating is that here, in Ancient Egypt, more than 3,000 years ago, we have most of the elements of a modern army, so far as its organization is concerned. And always, when you have such a large force of fighting-men you must also have ancillary services to maintain them in fighting-trim; to make and supply their weapons and equipment, to supply their rations and to pay them (though we do not know how this was done, since the Egyptians did not have coinage or money as we understand it).

As a humorous contrast to the pompous official descriptions of military campaigns, here is part of a sarcastic letter written by an old scribe, who had known military service, to a vain young colleague who had been appointed an 'army scribe' and had become rather swanky about it. An army scribe was an administrative officer who rarely took part in the fighting. They were of various ranks; 'army scribe', 'scribe of the infantry', 'scribe of assemblage' and 'scribe of distribution'. Like their modern counterparts, these unfortunate half-civilian officers were often derided by the fighting-men who did not always understand their difficulties. The document dates from about 1500 BC.

The letter begins by outlining the scribe's difficult situation. His own auxiliary troops number 1,900 men, but there are also other contingents, Shardana, Kehek, Mashawasha, Negroes, in all about 5,000 men whom the 'scribe of the army' is responsible for feeding. He has rations to distribute consisting of bread, cattle and wine, but he has underestimated the amount of food required. 'The number of men is too great for you, and the provision is too small for them', says the letter, which goes on:

> You receive the provision, and it is placed in the camp. The army is ready and equipped; so divide it up quickly and give to each man his portion. The Bedouins (auxiliary troops) look on furtively and say (in their own language 'Sopher yode' meaning, sarcastically, 'O wise Scribe!').
>
> 'Mid-day is come; the camp is hot' they say to you. 'It is time to start. Be not angry, O commandant of the auxiliaries. We have yet far to march' they say. 'Why is there no bread?' they say. 'Our night-quarters are far off.'[3]

The harrassed scribe, whose name is Amenemope, in despair, orders some of the rebellious soldiers to be beaten, an unwise move, for, as they point out, the Ruler (that is the Pharaoh) will shortly be arriving, and they will then make their complaints direct to him. 'Come on, give us our food!' they shout. 'If you don't it won't be long before this unit will be getting a *new* scribe! It was not a good idea to beat us, comrade . . . Before long the Pharaoh will hear of it, and that will be the end of *you*!'

This passage, although meant sarcastically, probably contains a lot of truth. The fact that the troops, who have been underfed and then unjustly beaten, can complain to the Pharaoh himself and hope for satisfaction is proof that such rulers as Tuthmosis III, when on the march with their soldiers, could be fair-minded and just, not scrupling to punish their officers if they proved inefficient. If this is so, as I believe it was, it goes a long way to explain why the Pharaohs of the New Kingdom were so often victorious. They knew how to win the loyalty of their troops. But, of course, in the end, everything depended on the Pharaoh being a capable general, as Tuthmosis III undoubtedly was. If Amenemope had behaved in such a clueless way he would certainly have been reduced to the ranks or dismissed from the army in disgrace.

The account of Tuthmosis's victory over the King of Kadesh is recorded in the temple which the Pharaoh erected at Karnak near Luxor. Unlike most such accounts this one appears to be based on first-hand information from an eyewitness; it is less fulsome and vague than other accounts and, in the inscription, the King states that he employed what we would call a 'war correspondent', a scribe whose task was to describe these dramatic events as they happened, on a leather scroll which was deposited in the temple archives. Indeed, we know the actual name of this correspondent, Thaneni, whose tomb on the west shore of Thebes contains the following inscription;

I followed the Good God, Sovereign of Truth, King of Upper and Lower Egypt, Menkheperre (Tuthmosis III); I beheld the victories of the king which he won in every country. He brought the chiefs of Zahi (in Syria) as living prisoners to Egypt; he captured all their cities. . . . I recorded the victories which he won in every land, putting (them) in writing according to the facts.[4]

The great Annals of Tuthmosis, inscribed on the temple walls, are the world's first full account of a military campaign in which the strategy and tactics of the general in command (Tuthmosis himself) are clearly described. So clearly, in fact, that modern scholars have been able to draw up a plan of battle after carefully examining the ground on which the battle was fought. According to these investigations, notably by Mr H. H. Nelson,[5] Thaneni's account is completely accurate in so far as the topography of the land is concerned, apart from somewhat exaggerating the narrowness of the pass along which the Pharaoh's army marched before it engaged the enemy. It is therefore most probable that his description of the fight is equally accurate.

Towards the end of the eighth month in his twenty-second year Tuthmosis advanced from his frontier fortress at Tjel (near modern Kantara on the Suez Canal) and crossed the 'Gaza strip' of more recent memory, seizing Gaza, a city of the Philistines, on the anniversary of his accession to the throne of Egypt. Staying only one night in Gaza, which he had reached after a march of ten days, he began another ten-day march to a place called Yehem. This has not been definitely identified, but it must have been within easy reach of the village of Aruna, where the great army halted preparatory to crossing the mountains beyond which lay the enemy.

There were three possible approaches through the mountains, two easy but long, one shorter but dangerously narrow, and if the enemy were to come on the Egyptian forces strung out in column-of-route they could be cut to pieces. Now here is the account of the King's Council of War, as recorded by Thaneni. The Pharaoh opens the conference.

That vile enemy of Kadesh, he said, has come and entered into Megiddo, and he is there at this moment. He has gathered to himself the princes of all lands who were loyal to Egypt, together with (those from) as far as Naharin . . . Syrians, Kode-people, their horses, their soldiers, and their people. And he says (so they say) 'I will stand to fight against His Majesty here in Megiddo.' Tell me what is in your hearts.[6]

To which the officers of the Council replied;

How can one go upon this road which is so narrow? It is reported that the enemy stand outside, and have become numerous. Will not horse have to go behind horse, and soldiers and people likewise? Shall our own vanguard be fighting, while the rear stands here in Aruna and does not fight? Now there are two roads here. One road comes out at Ta'anach, and the other is towards the north side of Djefti, so that we would come out to the north of Megiddo. So let our mighty lord proceed upon whichever seems best to his heart. Let us not go upon that difficult road.[7]

But the young Pharaoh, probably because he had more up-to-date intelligence reports of the enemy's movements, decided to do the one thing which the King of Kadesh would *not* expect him to do, that was to take the narrow, shorter and dangerous road. But first he has to shame his officers into following them. So like Shakespeare's Henry V before Agincourt, he gives the doubters a free choice.

He tells them that he intends to take the Aruna road, the narrow and more difficult (though shorter) one. As for his followers, they may do as they please. He continues;

Let him of you who wishes go upon those roads you speak of, and let him of you who wishes come in the train of My Majesty. Do not let these enemies whom Re abominates say 'Has His Majesty proceeded along another road because he has grown afraid of us?' For that is what they will say.[7]

Humbly the officers reply: 'Thy father Amun prosper and thy counsel. Behold we are in the train of Thy Majesty wherever Thy Majesty will go. The servant will follow the master.' Although the Egyptians came under attack as the rearguard had almost reached the end of the defile, the enemy were obviously not expecting Tuthmosis to choose this route. They had expected him to take one of the easier roads, so that when he reached the mouth of the wadi he saw that their south wing was massed at Ta'anach on the edge of the plain, while the north wing was near Megiddo. As so often in warfare, audacity had paid off.

With the Pharaoh's vanguard now beginning to spread out across the plain the officers again address him;

Behold, His Majesty has come forth together with his victorious army and they have filled the valley; let our victorious lord hearken to us this once, and let our lord await for us the rear of his army and his people. When the rear of the army has come right out to us, then we will fight against these Asiatics and we shall not have to trouble about the rear of our army.[8]

Taking their advice this time, Tuthmosis waits until noon for the rest of the army to come through. Then he advances to the brook Kina, south of Megiddo, by which time it was seven in the evening. Again, in the scribe's description of nightfall and the preparations for attack next day, one is reminded of the night scene before Agincourt in *Henry V*; even the youth of the two kings is similar. Henry was 28 when he fought his first great pitched battle at Agincourt; Tuthmosis was probably about 23.

Then was set up the camp of His Majesty, and command was given to the whole army, saying 'Equip yourselves! Prepare your weapons! for we shall advance to fight that wretched foe in the morning!' Therefore the king rested in the royal tent, the affairs of the chiefs were arranged, and the provisions of the attendants. The watch of the army went about saying 'Steady of heart! Steady of heart! Watchful! Watchful!' Watch for life at the tent of the King. One came to say to His Majesty 'The land is well, and the infantry of the South and North likewise.'[9]

Then comes the account of the battle itself and the famous, oft-quoted description of the king in his armour, mounted on his war-chariot, leading his army into action.

His Majesty went forth in a chariot of electrum' (alloy of gold and silver) arrayed in his weapons of war, like Horus, the Smiter, lord of power; like Montu of Thebes, while his father, Amun, strengthened his arms.

Horus, the hawk-god, was one of the oldest emblems of kingly power; one remembers that Narmer himself called himself 'Horus'. Montu of Thebes was the son of Amun-Re, the state god of Thebes who was then principal god of Egypt. The description then goes on to explain how the royal army was ordered for battle, with the southern wing on a hill south of the brook Kina, the northern wing at the northwest of Megiddo, while the forces of the centre were led personally by the Pharaoh in his war-chariot. Unfortunately the ancient scribe does not tell us the course of the battle, but only that the Pharaoh won, that he 'prevailed against them'.

Then His Majesty prevailed against them at the head of his army, and when they saw His Majesty prevailing against them they fled headlong to Megiddo in fear, abandoning their horses and their chariots of gold and silver. The people (of Megiddo) hauled them up, pulling them up by their clothing, into this city; the people of this city have closed it against them and lowered clothing to pull them up into this city. . . .

Then follows a rebuke to the Egyptian Army for stopping to collect the spoils of battle instead of pursuing the foe in retreat and taking Megiddo.

Now if only the army of His Majesty had not given their hearts to plundering the things of the enemy, they would have captured Megiddo at this moment, when the wretched foe of Kadesh and the wretched foe of this city were hauled up in haste to bring them into this city. . . .

Tuthmosis, one imagines, was furious;

Then spake His Majesty on hearing the words of his army, saying 'Had you captured this city afterward, behold I would have given (rich treasure) to Re this day; because every chief of every country that has revolted is within it; and because it is the capture of a thousand cities, this capture of Megiddo. Capture ye mightily, mightily. . . .[10]

So Tuthmosis orders a huge wooden wall to be built around Megiddo to prevent anyone escaping. Cedars from the surrounding country must have been felled to build this wall, a big task for the army and one which must have made them regret bitterly not having taken the city at the first onrush when the foe was in retreat. A long siege followed – the wooden wall preventing any possibility of relief from outside, or escape from inside Megiddo, which was eventually starved into surrender. The plunder of the city was considerable, and was carefully itemized in the temple inscription at Karnak, because much of it went as tribute to Amun-Re.

With Megiddo taken and the enemy defeated or dispersed, Tuthmosis was able to take and plunder other cities in the Lebanon including Yenoam, Nuges, Herenkeru . . . and again follows a careful list of plunder; 1,796 male and female slaves with their children, flat dishes of costly stone and gold, various drinking vessels, gold in rings 'found in the hands of the artificers', a silver statue in beaten work, the head being of gold, chairs, foot-stools, tables of ivory and carob wood, and so on. The captured land was divided into fields 'which the inspectors of the royal house calculated, in order to reap their harvest'. Then follows a statement of the yield of this harvest, 208,200 fourfold *heket* of grain.

Two facts strike one in reading this and other campaigns recorded in the Annals of Tuthmosis III – seventeen campaigns in all, and all apparently successful. One is that the young Pharaoh showed generalship of a high order, making an unpopular decision and being proved right, and planning his attack in such a way that he chose his own ground and left the enemy at a disadvantage. In all probability the battle was won before a single arrow was fired and Tuthmosis knew this when he arrived on the plain after his hazardous march through the narrow pass, and saw that the enemy, who had expected him by a different route, were disadvantageously placed for a pitched battle; but by then it was too late.

The second fact is by the time of the New Kingdom warfare was becoming a very profitable operation, if one won. No doubt the Tuthmosid kings were aware that while it was possible for

the 'vile Asiatics' to form alliances against them Egyptian possessions and trade outlets in Palestine would not be safe, and there
might come a time when Egypt's frontiers might again be threatened. Hence they were right to take the offensive. But the attractions of rich plunder also came into it; and the plunder, unlike
that of Nubia and Kush, included very beautiful and valuable
manufactured goods, let alone exotic foreign women who were
brought back in droves to Thebes. Some of these girls were
princesses, and married into the royal family and their court, and
this in time led to religious and social changes when the blood of
these foreign ladies mingled with that of the Pharaohs, because
they brought foreign ideas with them. We shall see some of the
effects of this in a later chapter.

Tuthmosis III has been called 'the Napoleon of Ancient Egypt'
with some justice. He was without doubt the most brilliant fighting general she ever produced, and his example inspired some of
his great successors such as Sethi I, and Ramesses II and III.
Although we have to rely for most of our information on the
stilted priestly chronicles, concerned more with recording the loot
for the temple of Amun-Re than describing the Pharaoh's person-
ality and achievements, a hint here and there suggests a generous,
warm-hearted as well as a brave and skilful man. His record is not
stained with massacres and other atrocities; he frequently shows
mercy to the inhabitants of captured towns, and his troops evidently adored him, to judge by the way they followed him loyally
almost to the ends of what to them was the world. It took a great
deal of courage for the Ancient Egyptian, accustomed for some
1,500 years to the closed society of the Nile Valley, to venture out
into the high mountains of Syria, and even to cross the mysterious
Euphrates, which, contrary to the Nile, flowed southwards instead
of northward. So they had to give it the quaint title of 'the river
which in flowing southward flows northward'.

Tuthmosis acquired a number of foreign wives from Asia, including three princesses bearing the charming names of Menhet,
Menwi and Merti. Some years ago 'illicit diggers' operating near
Luxor found their tomb, and robbed it, feeding the 'grave-goods'
on to the market at intervals. Among these objects are three sets

of toilet articles of gold, silver and other precious materials now on view at the Metropolitan Museum of Art, New York. They are illustrated (Plate 19) and were no doubt gifts from the King. As far as we know, the only woman he thoroughly detested was his aunt and stepmother Hatshepsut. After her death he defaced her monuments, cutting out her sculptured reliefs wherever he found them, defacing her royal name and substituting either his own or those of his predecessors Tuthmosis I and II. He even desecrated the tombs of her favourites, especially that of Sen-en-mut. But no doubt he had very good reasons for this hatred.

So it was that in later times even the records of this queen's reign as regent to Tuthmosis were obliterated, and instead the name of Tuthmosis II is followed, on the records, by that of Tuthmosis III, 'Menkheperre, the scourge of the Asiatics'.

---

[1] Breasted, J. H., *Ancient Records of Egypt,* Vol 2, Chicago University Press, 1906

[2] Gardiner, A. H., *Egypt of the Pharaohs,* Clarendon Press, Oxford, 1961

[3] Breasted, J. H., op. cit.

[4] Breasted, J. H., op. cit.

[5] Nelson, H. H., *The Battle of Megiddo,* Chicago

[6] Gardiner, A. H., op. cit.

[7] Gardiner, A. H., op. cit.

[8] Gardiner, A. H., op. cit.

[9] Breasted, J. H., op. cit.

[10] Breasted, J. H., op. cit.

7 Thebes Triumphant

It was during the reign of Tuthmosis III – 'Menkheperre' as he was also called (each Pharaoh had several names) – that the armed forces of Egypt reached the peak of their fighting power and efficiency, Moreover, unlike some of the Pharaohs of later dynasties. Tuthmosis did not use foreign mercenary soldiers to bolster his power. His army was a truly Egyptian army, though including, at times, auxiliary troops from Egyptian dependencies in Nubia and Palestine. These, however, were by now as much a part of Egypt as the Nile Valley; they were not foreign soldiers hired for pay. In fact, at this period the troops who fought under the Pharaoh's standard might be compared with the auxiliary troops who served in Rome's armies in much later times, troops who, though they came from Spain, or Syria, or Britain, as well as Italy, were still Roman soldiers.

What is particularly interesting is to see the way Menkheperre (*Men*-kepper-*ray*) overcomes tough military problems by the bold use of new techniques. Every campaign, and there were seventeen in less than thirty years, brought him new experiences which he applied in the next. For example, quite early on he decided to supply his armies in Palestine through the seaports on the east Mediterranean coast, and built at Memphis a great dockyard for building and equipping warships and transport vessels. While his son, the future Amenophis II, was still a youth, Tuthmosis sent him to this dockyard to get part of his training, which included naval as well as land warfare.

There is a record of this boy's early career on a stela found several years ago near the great Sphinx at Giza. Part of it reads as follows;

Strong was he of arms, one who never wearied when he took the oar; but he rowed at the stern of his falcon-boat as the best of two hundred men. After casting off when they had finished half an *iteru* (three-quarters of a mile) they were worn out and their bodies exhausted, nor could they draw breath any more. His Majesty, however, was mighty under his oar of twenty cubits (about thirty-three feet) in length. He cast off and finally moored his falcon-boat after completing three *iteru* (four and a half miles) in rowing without a rest from pulling the oar. The faces of the spectators were joyful at watching him. . . .

And so, I am sure, was his fond father, who, if he saw this achievement, would probably be responsible for erecting the stela. One can recognize the training which Tuthmosis gave his son in another passage from this inscription.

Now, moreover, when His Majesty was co-regent [that is, reigning jointly with his father in order to get experience of kingship] while still a fine young stripling, when he had developed his body (to maturity) and had completed eighteen years on his legs in valour, he was one who knew every work of Montu [the war-god] – there was no one equal to him on the field of battle. He was one who knew horses, without his like in the numerous army, nor was there one in it who could draw his bow. He could not be approached in fleetness.[1]

Returning to Tuthmosis III and his thorough preparations for campaigns, there was the famous occasion when he knew he would have to take his large army across the Euphrates in order to defeat the King of Mitanni. This was on his eighth campaign in the thirty-third year (about 1457 BC).

An inscription at Napata in Nubia tell us about this, and about one of the most remarkable feats accomplished by this most remarkable of Pharaohs. He began by establishing a camp in the neighbourhood of the Lebanese coast, a district famous for its cedars. There the Pharaoh caused to be built numerous 'boats' (probably rafts), which were then placed on wheeled wagons drawn by oxen. The inscription continues:

They (the boats) journeyed in front of My Majesty in order to cross that great river which flows between this country and Naharin (the Euphrates).

This extraordinary journey, across mountains and broad deserts, with a huge army and equipped with boats for the crossing, was something of which the Pharaoh and his people could well be proud.

He is a king to be boasted of [the inscription continues] in proportion to the performance of his two arms in battle – one who crossed the Euphrates in pursuit of him who attacked him; first of his army in seeing that vile enemy over the mountains of Mitanni, while he fled through fear before His Majesty to another far distant land. Then My Majesty set up a stela (boundary stone) on that mountain of Naharin taken from the mountain on the west wide of the Euphrates.[2]

If the route from Byblos ran through Katna, Tunip and Carchemish in northern Syria, this transportation of heavy boats by ox-wagon, over difficult roads, must have covered well over 250 miles. One can imagine the surprise and fear of the King of Mitanni when he saw that the Pharaoh had crossed the deserts of Syria bringing his own fleet with him! No wonder he was defeated and fled 'to another far-distant land' (likely enough the Hittites of Asia Minor, who later became one of Egypt's most powerful enemies).

On his long journey home Tuthmosis relaxed with his army in the 'marshes of Niy' on the Euphrates, hunting elephants. We know all about this from another source, the tomb of one of his veteran soldiers, Amenemhab. Like the two Ahmoses of El Kab, Amenemhab had his autobiography inscribed in his tomb, and there are a number of references in it to 'Menkheperre' and his adventures in far-off lands. The old warrior, naturally, is not backward in reciting stories of his own prowess; no Ancient Egyptian ever was.

Again I beheld another excellent deed which the Lord of the Two Lands did in Niy. He hunted 120 elephants, for the sake of their tusks. I engaged the largest which was among them, which fought against His Majesty; I cut off his trunk . . . before His Majesty, while I stood in the water between two rocks. Then my lord rewarded me with gold. . . .[3]

On the same campaign, during the siege of Kadesh, the ruler of that city used a cunning trick which he may have learned from the horse-rearing Mitanni. Now that horses, including many stallions, were used in chariot warfare, the distraction of a mare sent amongst them could produce chaos. Amenemhab relates how;

The prince of Kadesh sent forth a mare before the army, in order to (distract?) them; she entered among the army. I pursued after her on foot, with my sword, and I ripped open her belly; I cut off her tail, I set it before the king; while there was thanksgiving to god for it!

And at the final assault on Kadesh, Amenemhab was among the foremost, so he tells us.

His Majesty sent forth every valiant man of his army, in order to pierce the wall for the first time, which Kadesh had made. I was the one who pierced it, being the first of the valiant; no other before me did it. I went forth, I brought off 2 men, lords, as living prisoners. Again my lord rewarded me because of it. . . .[4]

Tuthmosis III died in the fifty-fourth year of his reign, and was buried not far from his father's tomb in the Valley of the Kings. His sepulchre can still be seen today, approached by a steep shaft cut in the rock, leading by many twists and turns, over a pit intended to deceive the tomb robbers, to the inner, secret burial chamber adorned with wall-paintings depicting the Pharaoh's journey through the Twelve Caverns of the Night with the god Osiris, and across the sky by day in the sacred boat of the sun-god Amun-Re. That was to be the height of his felicity in the afterworld, to accompany the sun-god, whose son he believed himself to be. The tomb contains no references, in its inscriptions, to the military achievements of this mightiest of the Pharaohs. What we know about those achievements we derive from the Annals in the Karnak temple, from various stela set up in Egypt and outside it, and from the tomb biographies of some of his comrades-in-arms.

It is by no means the largest and most magnificent of the royal tombs; those of the later kings, for example the Ramesses, are much bigger and are nowadays frequently visited by thousands of tourists. They are lit by electricity and loud with the clamour of guides' voices. But with the exception of one Pharaoh, Sethi I of the Nineteenth Dynasty, there is not one of these kings who, in his lifetime, equalled Menkheperre in military skill, courage, intelligence, and the extent of his power. To see Tuthmosis's tomb, with its small entrance in a remote part of the valley, one has to borrow an electric generator or carry candles or torches, for few tourists visit it, or even know of its existence.

This is probably as he would have wished it, because one can see the tomb in silence, and, looking down at the fine carved sarcophagus, feel more closely in touch with its long-dead owner. The sarcophagus is, of course, empty, like all except one of the royal sarcophagi which have survived in the Valley of the Kings, because this tomb, like nearly all the others, was robbed in antiquity. But by a miracle the body of the king has survived, and can be seen today in the Archaeological Museum in Cairo, in a room set apart for the royal mummies. Although the face has decayed, one can recognize it from its many sculptured portraits; a small, rather chubby face, not unkindly, but with a suggestion of humour in the lips. And the body is that of quite a small man, like Napoleon, with whom Tuthmosis III has been justly compared. A tiny, brown, shrunken corpse, swathed in wrappings, which once fought seventeen campaigns and conquered most of the then-known world.

Tuthmosis's successor was Amenophis II, the young man who had excelled so well at the oar of his 'falcon-ship', on the field of battle with his father, and after the latter's death, as a fighting Pharaoh in his own right, 'one who knew horses, without his like in the numerous army, nor was there one in it who could draw his bow'. Evidently he inherited his father's fighting qualities, nor was there any hope for the more indolent courtiers in Thebes that they would have an easier time once the new Pharaoh was seated on the throne of Egypt.

But the main impression one gets from the various accounts of his reign is of someone less balanced than his father. Sir Alan Gardiner comments that 'so far as it can be understood he seems while drinking to have given free expression to his contempt for foreign enemies, declaring the northerners, including "the old woman of Arpakh" and the people of Takhsy to be a useless lot, but he orders his viceroy in Nubia to beware of people there and their magicians, and urges him to replace any objectionable chief by some man of humble birth. A typically Egyptian combination of naivete and boastfulness!'[5]

Amenophis was not only a powerful oarsman; he was an archer

who had practised long under tutors specially appointed by his father. In the same Giza stela which describes his prowess with a 33-foot oar, there is this account of his skill as an archer.

He drew three hundred stiff bows, comparing the workmanship of the artisans who made them, in order to distinguish the ignorant from the clever. And he came also and did the following, which I wish to call to your attention. He entered into the northern garden and found set up for him four targets of Asiatic copper of a span (three inches) in their thickness and with twenty cubits (nearly 35 ft.) between one pole and its fellow. Then His Majesty appeared in a chariot like Montu in his power. He seized the bow and grasped four arrows at once. He rode northward, shooting at the targets like Montu in his regalia. His arrows came forth from the back of the one target while he attacked the next. And that is a thing indeed which had never been done nor even heard of in story; that an arrow shot at a target of copper came forth from it and dropped to earth, excepting at the hand of the king, rich of glory, whom Amun had strengthened.[6]

It is usual and right for sons to try to emulate their fathers, and when one is the son of Tuthmosis III the effort required is tremendous. Many times, when he was a 'stripling', Amenophis II must have stood in the temple of Amun-Re at Karnak and heard the priests intoning the great hymn in praise of his father. Even translated into English the rhythms of which are far removed from those of Ancient Egyptian, this hymn has a poetic splendour which causes the spine to tingle; the God Amun is addressing Tuthmosis.

I have come to cause thee to trample the chiefs of Djahi; I disperse them, beneath thy feet throughout their lands.
I have caused them to see thy Majesty as lord of rays; thou shinest before them in my image.
I have come to cause thee to trample the dwellers of Asia; so smitest though the heads of the Asiatics of Retenu.
I have caused them to see thy Majesty adorned in thy regalia
When thou takest the weapons of war in the chariot
I have come to cause thee to trample the Orient; so treadest thou the inhabitants of God's Land.
I cause them to see thy Majesty like a comet that streweth its flames and unfoldeth its train.
I have come to cause thee to trample the Occident; Keftiu and Isy are subject to thy dignity.

I cause them to see Thy Majesty as a young bull firm of heart and sharp of horns, wholly unassailable.[7]

There is one obvious exaggeration in this poem, of which only part is quoted. The 'Keftiu' mentioned in the last verse were the Minoans of Crete, an independent and powerful maritime power with whom the Egyptians had only trade relations. They would have been amused and indignant to know that the writer who composed Tuthmosis's laudatory hymn claimed Crete among the Pharaoh's conquests. Nevertheless, there is no doubt that he did conquer the Asiatic powers of Djahi, Retenu, Mitanni and 'God's Land'; there is independent evidence to support these claims. But there is one interesting point; whoever composed the hymn knew about the Minoan cult of the Bull, hence the reference to the 'young bull firm of heart'.

Amenophis II, in the seventh year of his reign, attacked the town of Shamash-Edom, which was about a day's march from Katna, i.e. about eleven miles from the Syrian town of Homs. Then, turning east, he crossed the river Orontes, as his father had done – 'over water turbulent like the god Rasaph' (a storm-god), the inscription informs us. Turning to survey the rear of his army, he noticed some of the enemy troops who had stolen up unseen from the town of Katna and were preparing to attack the Egyptian rearguard. The ancient writer tells us, in typically florid style, how the Pharaoh 'pounced upon their back like the flight of the divine falcon, and they gave way, their hearts fainting, each one fallen upon his fellow . . .' No doubt Amenophis was accompanied by his bodyguard, picked charioteers, but the inscription would have us believe that he destroyed his enemies single-handed. 'There was none with His Majesty save himself and his strong right arm. His Majesty slew them with a shot.'

This was on the first stage of an expedition sent to punish the Kings of Naharin and Mitanni, on the northern Euphrates, who had revolted when news reached them of the death of the formidable Menkheperre. Amenophis II was evidently as energetic a commander as his father, and probably more ruthless. Losing no time after the capture of Shamash-Edom, he advanced swiftly north-eastward towards the Euphrates, following the roads his father had trodden so often. On the way he captured seven rebellious rulers of 'the land of Tikshi' (probably near Kadesh) and only fourteen days after crossing the turbulent Orontes arrived at the town of Niy. It was near this city that Tuthmosis had hunted 120 elephants. The town opened its gates to the young Pharaoh and it is stated that the men and women acclaimed him enthusiastically from the city walls.

Unlike Tuthmosis III, who was small and stocky, Amenophis II was a man of powerful physique, as his mummy shows; one need not doubt the stories of his prowess at the oar and with the great bow, shooting from a speeding chariot. In his bronze body-armour and glittering war-helmet, as he stood erect in the gold and silver-mounted chariot, he must have been a magnificent and kingly spectacle. His vanity concerning his bowmanship found expression when, after arriving at Kadesh, he entertained some of the local princes by exhibiting his skill:

His Majesty shot next at two targets of copper in their presence on the south side of the town, and they made excursions at Rebi in the forest, and brought back numberless gazelles, hares, and wild asses.

He seems to have enjoyed single combat, the lonely, daring attack which would bring him personal glory in the eyes of his troops, as when an inscription states;

His Majesty proceeded on his chariot to Khasabu, alone and without a companion, and returned thence in a short time bringing sixteen living Maryannu at the side of his chariot, twenty hands (of slain enemies) at the foreheads of his horses and sixty cattle driven in front of him. Submission was made to His Majesty by this town. Now as His Majesty was going south in the Plain of Sharon [mentioned in the Book of Isaiah] he found a messenger of the prince of Naharin carrying a clay tablet (i.e. a letter) at his neck and took him as a living prisoner at the side of his chariot.[8]

Amenophis II returned to Memphis in triumph 'with joyful heart like a victorious bull'. Then follows the usual list of plunder which included over 2,000 captives, men and women, among whom were female musicians 'together with their instruments of silver and gold', 820 horses, 730 chariots and other arms, and the inscription ends with the rather charming comment that on his return from victory the Queen and her daughter 'saw the victories of His Majesty', presumably from a balcony in Thebes where they watched the royal procession.

Amenophis fought a second great campaign in the ninth year of his reign. The accounts of his victories, the taking of cities, and his valour in combat become monotonous through familiarity, especially as they are usually couched in the same terms by the scribe responsible for recording them. Now and again, however, one episode stands out from the rest, as when, after taking many prisoners and plunder, the army surrounded them with two ditches filled with fire, to prevent them escaping at night. And according to the report the Pharaoh himself kept watch over them all night, attended only by his personal servants.

After this second campaign, and another in Nubia, where he established his frontier beyond the fourth cataract, Amenophis does not seem to have done much fighting for the remaining fourteen years of his reign. He had no need to, if one is to believe the statement that after his last campaign in Palestine even the far-off kings of Naharin and 'great Khatti' (the Hittites of Asia Minor) were eager to send tribute.

He died in about the twenty-fourth year of his reign and was buried in a sumptuous tomb in the Valley of the Kings, not far from those of his father and grandfather. His successor, Tuthmosis iv, though he fought some minor campaigns, did not distinguish himself, and died after reigning for only eight years. He was the last of the Warrior Pharaohs of the Eighteenth Dynasty, of whom Tuthmosis iii was indisputably the greatest, in fact a military genius fit to be compared with Hannibal, Julius Caesar, Marlborough and Napoleon. Egypt never saw his like again, though there were some redoubtable fighting Pharaohs yet to be born. But he, together with his father and grandfather, were mainly responsible for transforming Thebes from a mere provincial city, in a remote part of Egypt over 600 miles from the Delta, into the richest and mightiest capital of the ancient world. More than that, these warrior kings of Thebes restored to Egypt the self-respect she had lost during the Hyksos occupation; they made her prosperous again, richer even than she had been in the days of the Old Kingdom Pharaohs. For she was now a 'world power'.

---

[1] Steindorff and Seele, *When Egypt Ruled the East,* Chicago University Press (paperback edition Phoenix Books)

[2] Gardiner, A. H., *Egypt of the Pharaohs,* Clarendon Press, Oxford, 1961

[3] Breasted, J. H., *Ancient Records of Egypt,* Vol. 2, Chicago University Press, 1906

[4] Breasted, J. H., op. cit.

[5] Gardiner, A. H., op. cit.

[6] Steindorff and Seele, op. cit.

[7] Steindorff and Seele, op. cit.

[8] Gardiner, A. H., op. cit.

8 What the Soldiers Thought About It

When we read these ancient records and are told that 'His Majesty raged like a panther', or that he 'came forth together with his victorious army and . . . filled the valley' or 'went forth in a chariot of electrum, arrayed in his weapons of war', one is reminded of the heroes of Homer's poems the *Iliad* and the *Odyssey*. Always the great man, king or chieftain or hero, stands well in the foreground, shining in splendid armour 'like the sun'; and somewhere in the background of the picture are masses of ordinary common soldiers and their slightly less common officers, the 'greatest of 50', the 'standard-bearer', the 'troop commander' and so on.

If you think about it, this is quite understandable. Most of these events were described or inscribed long after they took place. As stories they would have more appeal if they centred around the leaders, the Great Ones. Listeners and readers like to identify themselves with the hero of a story, and how much more interesting to identify with Achilles or Tuthmosis III than with the ordinary foot-slogging soldier! Especially for the foot-slogging soldier himself who, having been in the battles, alongside thousands of his comrades, would be far more interested in knowing what his leaders had been up to at the time. Hence the popularity of War Memoirs today.

With us it is different. Most of us, I believe, would be ready to give up quite a lot of Pharaonic victory stelae for the chance of reading one first-hand account by a charioteer or an infantryman of what it was *really* like at the battle of Megiddo, or during a long march over the Lebanese mountains, when one had to un-hook the chariot, dismantle and *carry* it where no roads existed. Did the Ancient Egyptian soldier approach his task with the same mixture of ribald self-mockery which one finds in Western armies today – a deliberately anti-heroic attitude which alone makes the strains of campaigning bearable? When we read about Falstaff's companions Nym, Bardolph and Pistol – rogues one and all – we love them partly because we tend to think that their cynical real-ism concerning courage and cowardice are somehow part of the Anglo-Saxon attitude. But is it? It comes as something of a sur-prise to find that when the lower-ranking Ancient Egyptian soldier is allowed to speak, his attitude was just as anti-heroic, though there can be no doubt of his fighting qualities. After all, it was the thousands of ordinary soldiers who followed Tuthmosis, who won his victories, and no doubt died for him, too. There is – apart from the doubtful case of Sekenre – no example of a Pharaoh who was ever killed in battle.

Our source is the story of the scribe Amenemope (*Ah*-men-*em*-o-pee) whom we met in Chapter 4 having great difficulty distri-buting the rations. There is a great deal more about him in the wonderful papyrus which has come down to us from the New Kingdom. It has often been quoted because it is practically the only record we have of soldiering in Ancient Egypt which mocks at war and those who have to practise it. The document takes the form of a long letter from an old scribe who has seen military action, poking fun at the pretensions of a young soldier, probably a very junior officer who has been boasting to his old master about what he intends to do on the field of battle. One imagines that Amenemope has only recently joined the army. The word '*mahir*' which occurs frequently means 'hero' and is meant sarcastically in this letter. Unfortunately we do not possess Amenemope's letter to which this is the reply, but it must have been very boastful to have annoyed the old scribe so much.

He begins by sarcastically reproving the young man for his boastful letter which is full of 'great words' and 'abounds in thrusts'. 'Very well', he says in effect, 'let us see what you know.'

'I am a scribe, a *mahir*,' you say again. There is truth in your words, say well. Come forth, that you may be tested.

A horse is harnassed for you, as swift as a jackal . . . and it is like unto a storm of wind, when it goes forth. You loosen the reins and seize the bow. We shall see what your hand will do. I will expound to you the nature of a *mahir* and show you what he does.

Have you not gone to the land of Khatti (land of the Hittites) and have you not seen the land of Upe? (near Damascus). Khedem – do you know the nature of it, and Igedii too, what is it like? Sumer of Sesse – on which side of it lies the town of Kher. . . ? What is its stream like? Have you not marched to Kadesh and Tubikhi? Have you not gone to the region of the Bedouins with the auxiliary troops of the army?

Have you not trodden the road to Meger, where the sky is dark by day, and is overgrown with cypresses and oaks, and with cedars that reach high heaven? There are more lions there than panthers and hyenas, and it is girt about with Bedouins on every side.[1]

The old scribe, whose name was Hori, then enjoys one of the favourite pastimes of old soldiers, trying to scare the young recruit with the perils he will have to undergo. Then he gives a whole list of names of places which *he* had known in former campaigns, but which the young man has almost certainly never heard of; and he gives us a wonderfully vivid picture of crossing rough mountain tracks with a chariot.

Have you not climbed Mount Shewe? Have you not trodden it, while your hands are cut and your chariot is battered by the ropes as your horse is dragged? You shrink from climbing it and prefer to cross by the stream. You now realize how it tastes to be a *mahir*, when you carry your chariot on your shoulder. . . . And when you come to a halt in the evening your whole body feels crushed . . . your limbs are broken.

But the troubles of Amenemope are only beginning. Awakened in the middle of the night, he finds that the camp has been raided, and everywhere there is confusion.

You are alone to do the harnessing, brother comes not to brother [your comrades are too busy to help you], the fugitives have come into the camp, the horse has been let loose, the camp has been ransacked in the night, and even your clothes are stolen. . . . Your groom has awakened in the night and marked what the thieves have done. He has taken what was left and joined them. He has mingled with the tribes of the Bedouins and become an Asiatic . . . *Now* you are a fully equipped mahir.[2]

There is a wonderful passage describing the trembling *mahir* crossing a narrow mountain defile, with the enemy hidden all around him.

Behold, there is the narrow defile, made perilous by Bedouins, who are hidden beneath the bushes; some of them are of four cubits and five cubits from the nose unto the sole of the foot, fierce of face, their hearts not mild, and they hearken not to your coaxing.

You are alone, no helper to go with you, and no army behind you. You cannot find a guide to show you a way of crossing. You determine to go forward, though you don't know the way. Shuddering seizes you, the hair of your head stands on end, your soul lies in your hand. Your path is full of boulders and shingle, there is no passable track, for it is all overgrown with . . . thorns, *neh*-plants, and wolfs-pad. The ravine is on one side of you, the mountain rises on the other. On you go and guide your chariot beside you, and fear that the horse will fall. If your horse falls down your 'hand' [part of the chariot, purpose not known] falls and is left bare, and your leather falls. You unharness the horse, in order to repair the 'hand' in the middle of the defile. You are not expert in the way of binding it, and you don't know how to fasten it together. The . . . falls from its place and the horse is already too heavily laden to load him with it. The sky is open, and you fancy that the enemy is behind you. Ah, that you had a hedge of . . . that you might put it upon the other side! Your horse galled up to the time you find quarters for the night. You perceive how pain tastes. . . .[3]

The rest of this painfully funny story tells how Amenemope, having arrived at the enemy town of Joppa, is befriended by a 'fair maiden that keepeth watch over the vineyards' who hides and consoles the young Egyptian officer. But one day he is recognized and betrayed. He is put on trial 'and your tunic of good Upper Egyptian linen, you sell it' (to bribe his way out of captivity). Then follows the perilous journey home.

You sleep every night with a piece of woollen cloth about you . . . you slumber and are inert. Your bow, knife and quiver are stolen, and your reins are cut in the darkness. Your horse has gone. . . . You stumble on over the slippery ground. The road stretches out before it. It smashes your chariot and your weapons fall to the ground and are buried in the sand.

Bitterest blow of all, when at last Amenemope succeeds in reaching Egypt, and says, 'Give me food and water, for I have arrived safely . . . they turn a deaf ear, they do not listen, they pay no heed to your tales.' All this is exaggerated, of course, but who can doubt that old Hori, drawing on a lifetime of experience in war, is telling the truth, though, in order to make a better story, he has put together all the calamities which could possibly befall a raw young charioteer? Even the ending is funny, when, after at last reaching Thebes and home, the young man 'makes his way to the smithy'.

> The workshop surrounds you. Smiths and cobblers are all about you. They do all that you wish. They attend to your chariot, and it ceases to be slack. They . . . are cut aright; its . . . (word unknown) is adjusted. They place leather (reins) in your hand. They put your yoke to rights . . . they give you a whip.[4]

Then, watched ironically by the palace workmen, who have either repaired his battered chariot or more likely provided him with a new one, Amenemope drives furiously along the streets of Thebes to show off to his friends. There can be no other meaning to Hori's final words; 'Forth you go quickly to fight on the field of battle, to accomplish deeds of valour. . . .'

Of course, even this is not the account of a common soldier's experience of war. If Amenemope had not been an officer, handsomely equipped, he would not have been able to buy his freedom by exchanging his fine tunic of Egyptian linen. And, come to think of it, it speaks well of his Bedouin captors that they agreed to this price instead of killing him and taking his possessions, as they could have done. Again he must have been tough and quick-witted, and probably knew the language of his captors; Hori's story is peppered with bits of Syrian dialogue, odd words of the Semitic tongues, rather like a soldier of the Second World War who picks up scraps of Arabic.

For the ordinary soldier, if he escaped death on the battlefield and struggled home wounded or sick, his fate is well described in the words of another scribe, adjuring his pupil not to become a soldier;

> Come, let me tell you how he goes to Syria, and how he marches over the mountains. His bread and water are borne upon his shoulders like the load of an ass; they make his neck as that of an ass, and the joints of his back are bowed. When he reaches the enemy he is like a trapped bird, he has no strength in his limbs. If he comes home to Egypt he is like wood that is

worm-eaten. He is sick and becomes bedridden . . . O scribe Ennana, turn
away from the thought that the soldier is better-off than the scribe . . .[5]

And yet many thousands joined the Egyptian Army, and by no
means all were conscripts, drafted into service. Any young man
who chose to be a scribe, which in our terms could mean many
things – tax-collector, clerk, book-keeper, civil servant – was
exempt from military service and taxation. (A 'scribe of the army'
was a kind of non-combatant soldier.) The very fact that the
schoolmaster scribe was so anxious to dissuade his pupils from
entering the army is proof that it must have considerable attractions for young men. What were the attractions?

The answer, if you look for it, is in that satirical letter from
Hori to Amenemope. Because if you look closely, reading
'between the lines', you can detect a note of pride behind the
obvious jeers. Hori emphasizes the hardships of a soldier's life
only to prove to his young colleague that he has endured them
and triumphed over them. And he felt more of a man for having
done so. It is, of course, wrong to romanticize warfare, but
military service, then and now, can bring its rewards; comrade-
ship in shared peril, a sense of purpose, of duty honourably
fulfilled; above all a sense of having defended something worth
defending, in this case the great civilization which the far-off
ancestors of the Ancient Egyptians had created out of the mud
of the Nile Valley. It is sometimes said that patriotism is relatively
a modern idea; I do not believe so. The impulse which drove so
many Egyptians to fight under the banners of Tuthmosis,
Amenophis, and later under Sethi I and Ramesses II, was not a
servile obedience to the Pharaoh's will. These men were proud of
their homeland and thought it well worth the risk of their lives to
keep it safe and prosperous. And there is, let us admit it frankly,
a glamour in being a front-line soldier. Why otherwise would the
cynical Hori thus describe the charioteer going into action?

A horse is harnessed for you, as as swift as a jackal . . . and it is like a
storm of wind when it goes forth. You loosen the reins and seize the bow.
We shall see what your hand will do.

Compare that passage with, say, Richard Hillary's description of flying a Spitfire in World War Two, or a modern jet-fighter pilot at the controls of a supersonic aircraft; the speeds are vastly different, but the spirit is exactly the same.

You might object that this, in itself, has nothing to do with the Warrior Pharaohs; surely, as gods, high above the common run of mankind, they did not even notice the gallantry of individual soldiers. But this is not true. There *was* a bond between the Pharaoh in his gold-embellished chariot, surrounded by his picked bodyguard of household troops, the 'Retainers of His Majesty', and the officers and men who fought under his command. You will remember how, in Chapter 5, 'The Fighting Tuthmosids', the officers who had served under Tuthmosid kings recorded in their tombs how they had received honours and promotion from the kings, who had 'observed their gallantry' in action. There were the two Ahmoses of El Kab, and there are examples of others which we have not mentioned.

Here is a rather touching story about one such officer, Amenemhab, the same Amenemhab who assisted Amenophis II at the elephant hunt, and killed the mare which had been sent into the ranks of the Egyptian charioteers to distract the horses. He had also fought under Tuthmosis III in his sixth campaign, when he captured Kadesh, in his eighth campaign when he fought three great battles in Naharin, and in his tenth, fourteenth and seventeenth campaigns. He must already have been advanced in years when Amenophis II, the great archer, came to the throne. But he happened to be one of the oarsmen rowing the royal barge, and the Pharaoh noticed the old soldier who records this moment in his tomb inscription.

His Majesty noticed me rowing wonderfully with him in his vessel [it is not clear whether the Pharaoh had taken an oar himself on this occasion, but one would not be surprised], 'Khammat' was its name. I was rowing with both hands at his beautiful feast of Luxor, likewise to the splendours of . . . I was brought to the midst of the palace; one caused that I should stand before the king Amenophis II. . . . I bowed down immediately before His Majesty; he said to me 'I *know thy character; I was abiding in the nest* [i.e. I was a child] *while thou wert in the following of my father. I commission thee with office that thou shalt be deputy of the army as I have said; watch thou the ēlite troops of the king*'. The deputy, Mahu, executed all that his lord said.[5]

A king who could recognize, among the rowers of the royal barge, an old soldier who had fallen on bad times, and so reward him with command of the household troops, was certainly not lacking in humanity.

---

[1] Erman, A., and Blackman, *The Literature of the Ancient Egyptians,* Methuen, 1927 (slightly modified by L. C.)

[2] Erman, A., and Blackman, op. cit.

[3] Erman, A., and Blackman, op. cit.

[4] Erman, A., and Blackman, op. cit.

[5] Erman, A., and Blackman, op. cit.

9 Ramesses the Magnificent

Everyone who has read about Ancient Egypt will have heard of Ramesses (*Ram*-a-sees), sometimes spelt Ramses or Rameses. Actually nine Pharaohs bore this great name, but most were only minor kings. The two greatest were Ramesses II and Ramesses III, of the Nineteenth and Twentieth Dynasty respectively. The conjectural dates of their reigns are Ramesses II (1290–1224 BC) and Ramesses III (1182–1151 BC). We have to say 'conjectural' because Ancient Egyptian records differ in the reign dates of the Pharaohs and no one can be absolutely certain when trying to compute their reigns in relationship with the birth of Christ. The dates I have quoted here and throughout this book are those of Sir Alan Gardiner.

We can, however, be certain of the approximate length of their reigns, because their mummified bodies have survived, together with those of most of the New Kingdom Pharaohs and doctors can tell us approximately how old these men were when they died. For instance, the reign of Ramesses III was a very long one and this is borne out by his mummy, which is that of a very old man. But you may find, when reading other books, that although the length of each reign is usually agreed between most scholars, they do not always agree as to the date on which each reign began.

But there is a big gap between the death of Tuthmosis IV (*c.* 1405 BC) and the accession to the throne of Ramesses II (*c.* 1290 BC) – a gap of 115 years. What happened in between those dates? They were very important years in Egypt's history, but apart from one Warrior Pharaoh, Sethi I (1309–1291 BC), not distinguished by the military prowess which had won such renown for Egypt under the fighting Tuthmosids. Tuthmosis IV was followed by Amenophis III, an idle, luxury-loving king with a beautiful wife, Queen Tiye, and an even more beautiful daughter-in-law, Nefertiti. She married the son of Amenophis III and Tiye, Amenophis IV, whose reign was marked by an extraordinary attempt by the young King to change the Egyptian national religion. Not only did he move his capital from Thebes to a new site now called Amarna, but he even changed his name from Amenophis to Akhenaten (Ak-en-*ah*-ten) after that of the One God, the 'Aten' which he wished all his subjects to worship.

Akhenaten's religious experiment, which some think was noble and others fatuous, does not concern us here, except in one important respect, the Pharaoh's attitude to warfare and the defence of his empire. Some authorities believe that Akhenaten was a pacifist, a man who would not fight even in defence of his country. Certainly his 'sole God, beside Whom there is none other' seems to have been a god of peace, unlike Amun, who gloried in the conquests of his son the Pharaoh. In the great Hymn to the Aten, which it is believed Akhenaten composed, only the gentle and benevolent aspects of the sun are emphasized, and the 'Aten' was either the disk of the sun or perhaps the life-giving power it radiates. The Hymn contains no reference to war, and throughout his reign there is no record of Akhenaten waging it. The only conflict was internal, and religious; between the rejected priests of the hated god Amun of Thebes and the zealous young reformer on the throne of Egypt. He even went so far as to order the name Amun to be hacked out of every monument where it appeared, and to this day you can see throughout Egypt evidence of his workmen's handiwork.

On the other hand, it would be rash, on this evidence alone, to say that this proves the Pharaoh to have been a pacifist, which means more than a lover of peace. It could well be that both he and his father, Amenophis III, felt so secure, thanks to the efforts of their warlike ancestors, that they could afford to relax and enjoy the fruits of peace, and the riches of their splendid and luxurious civilization. If they did think this, events were to prove them sadly wrong. If we had to rely only on the inscriptions carved on tombs and temples and stelae of this period, we might well imagine that all was well on the frontiers of Egypt. Fortunately, almost by a miracle, certain documents have survived which tell a very different story.

These are the famous 'Amarna Letters' discovered accidentally at Tell el Amarna (the site of Akhenaten's city) nearly 150 years ago. These little tablets of baked clay, about the size of large dog-biscuits, tell us more about the state of the Egyptian empire in the reigns of Amenophis III and Akhenaten (1405–1350 BC) than all the pompous official inscriptions. For they were confidential letters sent to the Pharaoh by foreign rulers and the hard-pressed governors of his Asian possessions. Here, for example, is one from a loyal governor named Ribbadi appealing to the King for help against a certain Aziru who was threatening one of the Pharaoh's Palestinian cities:

Behold Aziru has fought my chiefs, and the chiefs whom I despatched to the city of Simyra he has caused to be sized in the city. Both the city Beruta (Beirut) and the city Ziouna (Sidon) are sending ships to the city. All who are in the land of the Amorites have gathered themselves. . . . I need men to save the rebellion of this land. . . . Give me soldiers.

And in a slightly later letter the governor writes in indignation,

Grievous it is to say what he has done, the dog Aziru. Behold what has befallen the lands of the King on account of him; and he cried peace unto the land, and now behold what has befallen the city of Simyra – a station of my Lord, a fortress . . . and they spoil our fortress . . . ah, the cries of the place . . . a violent man and a dog . . .[1]

One might have thought that such appeals would have wrung the coldest heart, but it is only too clear from later letters from Ribbadi that no help was sent. In the end Byblos, the great and important seaport on the Lebanese coast, as rich as her sister-cities of Tyre and Sidon, fell to the enemy, and the governor had to flee. (The name of Byblos was then Gebaal)

Lo, it is not granted to my sons to take root of me, as the prophets have perceived of old. Behold my brother has commanded, he went out as my deputy. It is of no use, the soldiers of the garrison failed with him, and so the evil is done, and they made me flee from the city. It is not defended from the enemy. . . . Behold the city of Gebaal was a city truly like our eye; there was plenty of all that was royal in her midst. The servants of the chief city were at peace, the chiefs were our well-wishers when the King's voice was for all . . . It is the chief city of the land they have wasted for me. But the King my Lord will protect me, and restore me to the chief city, and to my house as of old.

O King my Lord, O King my Lord, save the city from shame. . . .

One cannot imagine Tuthmosis III, the great Menkheperre, allowing this to happen, or, had it happened, allowing it to go unavenged. But those were the days, as Ribbadi says, when 'the King's voice was for all', that is when the Pharaoh's mighty power was felt to the utmost limits of his empire, and not merely in Syria-Palestine. Things were very different under Akhenaten, when, in a letter which brings us the sound of the enemy at the very gates, Ribbadi had to write:

. . . march against him and smite him . . . The land is the King's land, and since I have talked thus and you have not moved the city has been lost. There is no money to buy horses, all is finished, we have been spoiled . . . give me thirty companies of horse with chariots, men, men . . . there is none of this for me . . . not a horse![2]

And yet, when that letter was written, Egypt was probably as rich as ever she had been. It was not lack of money, resources or men which held the Pharaoh back. Whether it was a deliberate policy of 'non-aggression' (or 'non-defence') or indolence and indifference history does not tell us. But obviously such a state of affairs could not last, and there must have been many people in Egypt who, knowing the truth about the state of the empire, would want to protest, even if at first they had to smother their hatred of Akhenaten and his counsellors. Among these murmurers would undoubtedly be the priests of Amun. In fact, it seems, certain that after Akhenaten's death, or perhaps even before it, a move was made towards a reconciliation with Thebes. We know that his successor, Smenkhkare – a mere boy – was transferred to Thebes, probably in an attempt to come to terms with the priests of the older faith. Smenkhkare reigned for only three years, and his successor, Tutankhamun, for nine. He, too, must have been a child when he came to the throne, as he died while still in his late 'teens; probably his name would have been forgotten but for the fact that the wonderful furnishings of his small tomb survived almost undisturbed down to the twentieth century – alone among over thirty Pharaohs, most of whom were of far greater importance than this boy-ruler.

With the death of Tutankh*amun* (originally named Tutankh*aten* – another indication that the Court had decided to abandon Akhenaten's new god) the Eighteenth Dynasty, which had begun so gloriously under Ahmose, flickered out like a spent candle. Admittedly there was one, possibly two more Pharaohs, but of these, King Ay appears not to have been of the royal stock, but may have gained his position by marrying Tutankhamun's young widow, Ankhesnamun, one of the daughters of Akhenaten; he was an elderly politician and did not live long. He was followed by a soldier named Horemhab, whom some regard as the last Pharaoh of the Eighteenth Dynasty while others think he was the founder of the Nineteenth. Sir Alan Gardiner places him between these two Dynasties. He, too, was not of the blood royal, and may have acquired his right to the throne by marrying Nefertiti's sister.

Horemhab is an interesting character. He was a soldier, and had been Akhenaten's Chief of Staff. As such he must have chafed under the inactivity which the Pharaoh's feeble foreign policy forced upon him. Stationed as he was at Memphis in the north (where his rifled tomb has been discovered), he must have been keenly aware of the dangers which had arisen in the north-eastern provinces. It was not merely a question of quarrels between petty chieftains such as Aziru and Ribbadi; behind these puppets was a much more powerful foe, the King of the Hittites. He made use of these disputes between the vassal-kings (petty chieftains) of Egypt's empire in order to increase his own growing power.

To the Egyptians the Hittites were the 'abominable Kheta'. In the Hebrew scriptures there are references to the 'Hittites' and the 'children of Heth', but these were not the original Hittites whom the Ancient Egyptians fought in the fourteenth century BC. By the time Kingdoms of Israel and Judea had been founded in about 1000 BC the great Hittite empire was a thing of the past.

The Biblical 'Hittites' were descendants of Hittite-speaking refugees who had settled in Syria and Palestine when their own homeland was invaded and they were driven out. Many were not even Hittites from Asia Minor, but subject peoples who had learned to speak the same language. Therefore we must dismiss the Biblical Hittites from our thoughts when we consider the formidable 'Kheta' whom Ramesses II fought at the Battle of Kadesh.

But Horemhab must have known about them, through his spies in Palestine and Syria. He knew, none better, that while the dreamer Akhenaten neglected the pleas of his foreign governors such as Ribbadi, the Hittite monarch with a vast army was moving slowly but relentlessly down from the high mountains of Anatolia (modern Turkey) through northern Syria, mopping up, one by one, the petty states which had owed their allegiance to the Pharaoh. The Hittites were a race of tough mountaineers, hardened by bitter warfare, who had defeated even the powerful state of Mitanni on the Euphrates, Egypt's old enemy and later her ally. The little Asiatic kingdoms of Syria, Palestine and the Lebanon were no match for those stocky, irresistible mountain troops in their conical hats and mountaineers' boots, with their massed infantry and powerful chariotry, all under the leadership of a king skilled in the art of war.

When, on the death of the Pharaoh Ay, Tutankhamun's successor, Horemhab became the Pharaoh, he seems to have tried, if ineffectively, to reassert Egypt's rights in the Lebanon and Palestine, but the task of reconquering the lands further north was beyond his resources. However, he may have achieved one doubtful distinction, that of preventing a dynastic marriage between Ankhesnamun, the widow of Tutankhamun, and the prince Zananza, son of the Hittite king Suppililiumas (*Sup*-il-ee-*lew*-mas), which, if it had occurred, would have made the Hittites masters of Egypt without striking a blow. Documents discovered at the Hittite capital of Boghaz-Koy in Turkey prove beyond doubt that the young queen was writing to Suppililiumas imploring him to send her one of his sons so that she might make him King of Egypt. Probably she did this because she did not wish to marry either Ay or Horemhab, who were rivals for the throne.

At first the Hittite king was suspicious, and naturally so, but eventually he sent the young prince to Egypt; or rather he intended to do so, but Zananza never got there. On the way he was killed by 'the men and horses of Egypt' – to quote the Hittite chronicle. Suspicion falls naturally on two men, Ay and Horemhab, but for a number of reasons, chiefly his position as Chief in Command of the Army, I think it was most probably Horemhab who ordered the killing, probably arranging matters so as to make it appear an accident. Egyptian chariot patrols would normally be on duty along the Egyptian frontier and what would be more natural than that the Hittite prince's *entourage* be mistaken for a band of marauding Bedouin?

Ankhesnamun's only hope of escaping an unwelcome marriage (and remember she was probably not more than 18 at the time) lay in marrying someone powerful enough to be a match for either of the scheming politicians, Ay and Horemhab, who were fighting for the throne. She failed; Ay seems to have married her and she disappeared from the scene. No one knows what happened to her. Ay was followed by Horemhab, who reigned for about twenty-seven years. With his death the Nineteenth Dynasty begins, in about 1308 BC.

The first king, Ramesses I, reigned for only two years. He had been one of Horemhab's old military commanders and was already old when he came to the throne. We do not know how he laid claim to it, probably through marriage to a royal heiress. In 1309 BC he was succeeded by one of the most remarkable men who sat on the throne of Egypt, Sethi I, whose magnificent tomb in the Valley of the Kings has awed visitors for more than 2,000 years. Compared with this superb sepulchre, those of Tuthmosis III and Amenophis II are modest houses; that of Tutankhamun is a rabbit-hutch. Although he reigned only for eleven years, he achieved so much distinction, both as a soldier and an administrator, that he may be regarded as one of the greatest of the Warrior Pharaohs.

After the disasters which has overtaken Egypt during the reign of Akhenaten, Sethi was careful to restore full honour to the ancient gods of Egypt, such as Amun-Re, Ptah, Seth (after whom he himself took his name), and Osiris, god of death and resurrection. At Abydos he built to Osiris a splendid temple which is one of the marvels of Egypt to this day. There are many inscriptions in Egypt which record what he did. For instance, one of the principal sources of Egypt's wealth was the gold mined in the neighbourhood of the Red Sea (see map). To reach this spot the miners had to traverse a stretch of waterless desert between the Nile Valley and the coast. It was said by one historian that only one-third ever got there; the rest died of thirst. So the Pharaoh, on one of his royal progresses, set up an inscription in the Wadi Abbad (a 'wadi' is a dried-up watercourse through the desert) telling how he 'stopped on the way' and thought of the plight of the miners. 'Surely their throats will be parched. What will slake their thirst?' The royal inscription goes on: 'The homeland is far away, the desert wide. Woe to him, a man thirsty in the wilderness.' So Sethi had a deep well dug at the spot 'so that future generations may bless my name in years to come . . . inasmuch that I am one compassionate and regardful of travellers.'

It is easy to sneer at this document on the grounds that the Pharaoh was more interested in the gold than in the welfare of those who dug for it. And this may be true. Yet the fact remains that no other Pharaoh of earlier ages had left such a monument; and there is something in the flavour of the wording which suggests, to this writer at least, that it was based on vivid personal experience and compassion.

As a soldier Sethi I *may* have been the equal of Tuthmosis III; it is difficult to say who was the greatest, since Sethi I reigned only for eleven years, and therefore did not have the time or opportunity to register his conquests as did Tuthmosis, who reigned for fifty-four years. Yet in those few years he achieved much. There is an inscription on the exterior north wall of the great Hypostyle Hall in the Karnak temple which shows the King's prowess in battle and gives some details of his campaigns in Syria. One inscription is accompanied by a sculptured relief showing the Pharaoh returning from battle with two Syrian prisoners, one tucked under each arm – a unique representation!

Looking back over a distance of some 3,000 years it is clear
that the general situation was not unlike that which followed the
invasion of the Hyksos, except that in this case Egypt had not
actually suffered foreign invasion and occupation. But there was
the same sense of frustration. The 'vile Asiatics' and their Hittite
supporters had gained control of the lands in the Lebanon,
Palestine and Syria which Egypt had grown accustomed to regard
as her own. Sethi I marched out of the frontier fortress of Tjel,
crossed the Sinai desert at a speed which would not have shamed
Menkheperre, and then reached the town of Raphia along a route
carefully marked with the many small fortified stations protecting
the wells. All this we know for certain because the description and
'route-map' are inscribed in the Hypostyle Hall at Karnak, the
earliest equivalent of a route-map known anywhere in the world.
Twenty miles beyond Raphia, Sethi came to what is described as
a 'town of Canaan' which is clearly Gaza. One is immediately
reminded of the first campaign of Tuthmosis III, in whose foot-
steps Sethi was treading. Near this town he inflicted tremendous
slaughter on the 'Shosu' – Bedouin tribesmen who tried to bar
his way. Sethi reached the coast of the Lebanon, as is clearly
shown in the temple reliefs, where we see native princes of that
country felling the tall cedars which are required for the sacred
barques and flagstaffs of Amun.

In the record of a later campaign Sethi reaches historic Kadesh
on the Orontes in Syria, the city against whose chieftain Tuthmosis
III had fought victoriously at the battle of Megiddo. Kadesh was
always a vital strong-point, because lying at the northernmost end
of the B'kaa Valley, it was a point which any Egyptian army had
to cross if approaching from the south along the valley – the
obvious route. Sethi claims to have inflicted a victory against the
Hittite king Mursilis II, the successor to Suppililiumas. Several
well-known Biblical names are mentioned in this record at
Karnak, including Yenoam and Bethshael. But what is much
more interesting is the description of the various army divisions
commanded by Sethi, each with its name;

Thereupon His Majesty sent the first army of Amun 'Powerful of Bows' to
the town of Hamath, the first army of Re 'Manifold of Bravery' to the town of

Bethshael, and the first army of Sutekh (Seth) 'Victorious of Bows' to the town of Yenoam. . . .³

Sethi I died in the year 1291 BC and was succeeded by the great Ramesses II, undoubtedly the most famous and best-publicized Pharaoh of them all. It is impossible to visit the monuments of Ancient Egypt and not be aware of Ramesses II. His colossal statue, removed from Memphis, greets the visitor when he leaves Cairo's main railway station. There is another, similar statue lying prone at Memphis itself. There are huge statues of Ramesses in the Luxor temple, in his funerary temple across the river, called the Ramesseum, and, most gigantic of all, the seated colossi at Abu Simbel which for some 3,000 years stared out across the river, hewn from the living rock, guarding the entrance to Ramesses' great underground temple. Now, saved from the rising waters piling up behind the new High Dam, they survey the huge lake which is gradually submerging all Nubia, its temples, its cities, and its fortresses.

Not content with erecting larger statues than those of any other Pharaoh, and enlarging the Karnak temple on a scale which makes human beings, crawling at the feet of its columns, look and feel like ants, he even 'usurped' (that is, took over, stole) the statues of his predecessors, cutting out their royal names and substituting his own. He was the greatest builder Egypt has ever known. He would like to be remembered as the greatest warrior king. But was he? One has to be careful here.

We in the twentieth century are well accustomed to the power of self-advertisement, the publicity 'gimmick', the 'big lie'. Certainly Ramesses II knew very well how to advertise himself and his achievements, which were memorable and worthy of praise. And just because many of us today are repelled by too much self-advertisement we may be unfair to this extraordinary man, who had so many advantages. Not only was he highly successful but he was also good-looking, if his artists do him justice; and one could hardly say the same of Tuthmosis III, with his little pudgy round face and stocky figure. But Tuthmosis was a greater soldier.

On the other hand, it is quite wrong to judge the Ancient

Egyptians by the standards of the present day, when we pretend that it is wrong to boast. Actually we are still boasting, only more subtly. The Egyptians saw no shame in it, as we have seen, and Ramesses II was just a bigger and more effective boaster than any other Ancient Egyptian king. This does not mean, however, that he did not do what he claims to have done. There is absolutely no proof that his boasts were lies, though he sometimes exaggerated.

It was during his reign that the long-anticipated clash between the historic Ancient Egyptian power and the newly risen Hittite empire took place. It was one of the decisive confrontations of history, and the Egyptians considered it so important that they devoted hundreds of square yards of wall space in their temples to celebrating what Ramesses regarded as his great victory over the Hittites at Kadesh. Not only was this scene repeated again and again in huge carved reliefs, but in deep-cut hieroglyphic inscriptions the royal scribes described every detail of the battle, including the dramatic moment when the Pharaoh's personal valour saved the day, and, according to the official story, won the Battle of Kadesh for the Egyptians.

Some people tend to sneer at this story, supposing it to be an invention, but I cannot believe that even Ramesses would cover the walls of his principal temples, for thousands to see, with a portrayal of an incident which never happened. After all, among those thousands there must have been many who were at the battle and would know whether or not it was true. I think we can be certain that the details of that historic struggle between the two great powers were as true for the Ancient Egyptians, and as much a subject for national pride, as the Battle of Thermopylae was for the Ancient Greeks. But whereas the Greeks were content to commemorate their victory with a simple monument, Ramesses II had to cover wall-space almost as big as the West Front of Salisbury Cathedral to immortalize his. Because we are more like the Greeks than the Egyptians, we prefer their simplicity to the Egyptians florid inscriptions. It is purely a matter of national temperament and religious belief. For Ramesses, remember, was a god.

The campaign began in the fifth year of Ramesses' reign (1285

BC), when the King, leading a powerful army of four crack
divisions, chariotry and infantry, crossed the frontier at a place
called Sile (*Si*-lee) somewhere north of what is now Ismalia, on
the site of the modern Suez Canal. His object was to meet and
destroy the forces of the Hittite king Muwatallis, grandson of the
great Suppililiumas, who was said to be encamped near Kadesh
on the Orontes. This city had so often been like a bone in the
throat of the Egyptians, the throat being the B'kaa Valley, the
main route into Syria. If you look at the map on page 4 you will
see why. Every Egyptian army moving northward into Syria had
to pass this way if it wished to avoid the narrow, tortuous coastal
route hemmed between the mountains and sea, with river mouths
intersecting it.

It was spring, the best season for campaigning, and the banners
of the divisions, of Amun, of Ptah, of Sutekh and Re waved
bravely above the ranks of marching men whose spear-tips caught
the sun, above the plumed horses and the glittering chariots;
column after column visible at a great distance by clouds of
desert sand kicked up by some 20,000 men. Near the front rank,
resplendent in glittering bronze armour, battle-helmet on his
head, Ramesses rode in what, we may be sure, was the most
magnificent chariot in all that splendid cavalcade, surrounded by
his officers. Most, like himself, were young men, though there
were also veterans who had fought under his father Sethi I and
even perhaps under Horemhab.

After a month's arduous marching over that harsh desert land
the army reached the forbidding mountains of the Lebanon range,
crossed it, and occupied a position on a ridge above Kadesh,
which was fifteen miles away. Next morning the eager young king
made an early start, descending, at the head of his own division,
(that of Amun), the 600-foot winding mountain track which
brought him down to the valley and the ford across the Orontes
at Shabtuna (modern Ribla). Here two Bedouin were brought
before him, claiming to be deserters from the army of Muwatallis.
They wanted to serve in the Pharaoh's army, they said, and on
being questioned stated that Muwatallis's army was far away in
the 'land of Khaleb' (near modern Aleppo) to the north of Tunip.

It is easy to say that the redoubtable Menkheperre (Tuthmosis III) would have been very cautious about accepting this welcome information, but Ramesses was young, and had not the great Menkheperre himself set an example of audacity in this very field of action? Had not he ignored the advice of his officers and marched his vanguard along a narrow, dangerous road in order to surprise the enemy? But in this case there seemed to be no enemy to surprise, if Muwatallis was as far away as Aleppo. Surely it was essential to waste no time, but to cross the Orontes and march northward as soon as possible? So the division of Amun, with Ramesses at its head, splashed through the ford, while messengers were sent urging the other three divisions to follow at all possible speed.

Even this was not fast enough for Ramesses. Leaving the rest of the division behind, he and his bodyguard advanced to a point some seven miles from the ford, where they set up camp to the north-west of Kadesh. What he should have done, we see now, was to wait until the rest of his divisions had arrived and reached the west bank of the river, and then advanced together with them. But Ramesses was young and relatively inexperienced.

One doubts if ever again he was so impetuous, because, just after he had seated himself on his golden throne at the last camping-place, two captured Hittite scouts revealed the unwelcome truth. The entire army of Muwatallis and his allies was hidden a little to the east of Kadesh, ready to do battle, while the divisions of Ptah, Re and Sutekh were still miles behind the King, in column of route, struggling to catch up with him.

I have been to the site of this battlefield. Nothing remains of the walled city of Kadesh. An undistinguished village of mud-brick huts occupies the site, and there is a broad tarmac road punctuated by telegraph-poles across the broad, flat valley floor. Yet it is still possible to imagine the scene as it must have appeared in 1285 BC, with the unprepared armies of Ramesses caught in the trap which the wily Muwatallis had prepared for them. Today the great valley is quiet save for the occasional car or lorry speeding past in a cloud of dust, or a string of laden camels moving softly past along the sandy verge of the road. The sun beats down on the purple mountains and the air quivers in the heat. Three thousand years ago, hidden in a fold of those mountains, the Hittite forces lay hidden until the moment when the Egyptian Army, still on the march, moved down into the valley.

Muwatallis had amassed a vast concourse of men. An Egyptian temple chronicler records a formidable list of names: 'the whole land of Khatti [in Asia Minor] had come, and likewise Naharin, Aradus, Pedes, Irun', etc., etc. It was a huge alliance of countries which the Hittite monarch had gathered around him to oppose Egypt. 'All their princes were with him, and every one of his foot soldiers and chariotry. . . . They covered the mountains and valleys and were like locusts in their multitude.'[4]

Then Muwatallis struck, and the whole valley was filled with the roar and clamour of his advancing legions. Probably that valley has never heard a louder thunder from that day to this, as some 70,000–100,000 armed men clashed in fury. Ramesses, at his advanced post, found himself cut off from his army. He claims to have been entirely alone, but in fact he must have had his bodyguard at least with him, otherwise he could not have survived such an onslaught. Probably he and his companions rapidly chose some point of vantage which gave some cover, and prevented them from being surrounded and overwhelmed. Then His Majesty fought from his chariot, like the fine soldier he was, until the Division of Amun and the Division of Re could get through to him, or he to them. The chronicle, which at this point becomes a poem, continues in these words:

Then His Majesty arose like his father Mont and took the accoutrements of battle, and girt himself with his corselet; he was like Baal in his hour, and the great pair of horses which bore His Majesty, belonging to the great stable of Usimare-setpenre, beloved of Amun, were named Victory-in-Thebes. Then His Majesty started forth at a gallop, and entered into the host of the fallen ones of Khatti, being alone by himself, none other with him. And His Majesty went to look about him, and found surrounding him on his outer side 2500 pairs of horses with all the champions of the fallen ones of Khatti and of the many countries who were with them; they were three men to a pair of horses as a unit, whereas there was no captain with me, no charioteer, no soldier of the army, no shield-bearer; my infantry and chariotry melted away before them, not one of them stood firm to fight with them. . . .

At this point it will be noted that the poet is writing as if in the person of the King, who addresses a prayer to his father the god Amun.

What ails thee, my father Amun? Is it a father's part to ignore his son? Have I done anything without thee, do I not walk and halt at they bidding? I have not disobeyed any course commanded by thee. How great is the great lord of Egypt to allow foreigners to draw nigh in his path! What careth thy heart, O Amun, for these Asiatics so vile and ignorant of God? Have I not made for thee very many monuments and filled they temple with my booty, and built for thee my Mansion of Millions of Years (Amun's temple) and given thee all my wealth as a permanent possession? . . . [and there is much more in this strain, including an elaborate list of temple offerings][5]

It must be remembered that this chronicle was drawn up by the priests long after the battle, and they were concerned mainly to show how important Amun was. It seems doubtful if Ramesses II, in the heat of the fight, would have either time or inclination to address more than a hasty prayer to his god. But eventually Amun comes to his aid and enables him to rout the foe single-handed, pushing them back into the river Orontes, where many drowned. As Sir Alan Gardiner observes, 'It cannot be doubted that the Egyptian king did display great valour on this momentous occasion, but both the "Report" and the sculptured scenes suggest that what saved Ramesses was the arrival, in the nick of time, of the youthful troops that had been mentioned earlier as stationed in the land of Amor; perhaps we should think of them as coming up from the neighbourhood of Tripoli along the road crossed by the Eleutheros river; at all events they attacked the Hittites in the rear and completed their discomfiture.'[6]

Before this timely arrival, however, Ramesses had to fight hard and repeatedly. Menna, his charioteer, lost heart and appealed to the King in these words:

'My good lord, valiant prince, great protector of Egypt in the day of battle, we stand alone in the midst of the foe. Behold, the foot-soldiery and chariotry have abandoned us. Wherefore wilt thou stay until they bereave us of breath? Let us remain unscathed, save us, Ramesses!'
Then said His Majesty unto his charioteer: 'Steady, steady thine heart, my charioteer. I shall enter in among them even as a hawk striketh; I slay, hew

in pieces, and cast to the ground. What mean these cowards to thee? My face
groweth not pale for a million of them.' His Majesty hastened forwards and
charged them until the sixth time. . . .

The battle lasted two days. On the second day Ramesses continues:

When the day dawned I began the fighting in the battle. I was ready for the
fray like a bull on the alert; I shone forth against them like Mont, furnished
with fighters and mighty men. I forced my way into the melee and fought even
as a hawk striketh. The royal snake upon my brow, it overthrew mine enemies;
it spat forth fire into the face of the foe. It was like Re when he ascendeth into
the morning, and my rays burnt the limbs of the enemy. One cried out to the
other 'Look to yourselves! Lo, the mighty Sekhmet [the lioness-headed
goddess] is with him; she is by him on his horses, and her hand is with him.
If any draweth nigh unto him, the blast of fire cometh and burneth his limbs.'
They began to kiss the ground before me. My Majesty was mighty behind
them, I made slaughter among them. They were cut to pieces before my steeds,
they lay together stretched out in their blood.[7]

And in a passage which occurs a little later in this epic poem
the defeated King of Khatti is represented as sending his envoy
(representative) to the victorious Pharaoh pleading for peace.
Muwatallis says that yesterday the Pharaoh 'didst slay hundreds
of thousands. . . . Be not severe in thine utterance. O mighty
king, peace is better than the strife of battle. Give us breath!'

What truth can be extracted from all this? We can disregard such
statements as 'thou didst slay hundreds of thousands' and also the
suggestion that Ramesses won the battle almost single-handed.
But there can be no doubt that the fight was decisive in that the
Hittite monarch advanced no further; if he had not suffered severe
losses, there was nothing to prevent him advancing on Egypt. On
the other hand, this cannot be regarded as a complete victory for
Ramesses. In the royal archives of Boghaz Koy, the Hittite capital,
documents were found in which the Hittites claimed the victory
at Kadesh. These chronicles, written under the direction of
Muwatallis's brother Khattusilis, state that Ramesses was conquered and retreated to the 'land of Aba' (near Damascus) and
was later replaced there by Khattusilis as regent.

Perhaps the basic truth is that the two great powers, after their trial of strength, realized that neither could overcome the other. Ramesses II remained King of Egypt, and continued to reign for a total of sixty-seven years, dying in 1224 BC. The civilization of the Nile Valley, which Hor-Aha, the 'fighting hawk', had unified and made strong more than 1,900 years earlier, had once again survived the attacks of its enemies. But never again would the Pharaoh enjoy undisputed control of all Syria. As for the Hittites, they signed a peace treaty with Ramesses in the twenty-first year of his reign, copies of which were kept at Karnak and also at Boghaz-Koy, where the Hittite version of the treaty was discovered by the German archaeologist Winckler over sixty years ago. Under the terms of this treaty of non-aggression, the clauses of which are almost identical in both Hittite and Egyptian versions, each power agrees not to attack the other and to come to the aid of the other party if attacked. Even the Queens of Egypt and Khatti exchanged greetings, and the alliance was cemented by the marriage of Ramesses to a Hittite princess. There is a wonderful statue of the royal pair in the Cairo Museum though the sculptured figure of the little Hittite lady hardly reaches the top of Ramesses calf. Such was the position of Egyptian queens of this period in relation to the King!

Within a hundred years the Hittite Empire had ceased to exist, destroyed by newcomers who invaded Asia Minor and forced the remnants of the Hittites to emigrate, many of them to Syria-Palestine, where one of their descendants, Uriah, served on the military staff of King David. But Egypt survived, almost, if not quite, as great as ever. All that the battle of Kadesh proved, in the end, is that 'peaceableness is better than the strife of battle'. It seems a pity that thousands of men had to die just in order to prove that neither side could win. But that is in the nature of war.

[1] Erman, A., and Blackman, *Literature of the Ancient Egyptians,* Methuen, 1927
[2] Erman, A., and Blackman, op. cit.
[3] Gardiner, A. H., *Egypt of the Pharaohs,* Clarendon Press, Oxford, 1961
[4] Erman, A., and Blackman, op. cit.
[5] Gardiner, A. H., op. cit.
[6] Gardiner, A. H., op. cit.
[7] Erman A., and Blackman, op. cit.

A relief on the wall of the Hypostle Hall in the Ramesseum at Thebes, showing the storming of the Hittite fortress of Zapur which the Egyptians are attacking with scaling ladders under the protection of shields   *Roger Wood*

Unfinished fresco in the tomb of Horemhab   *The Mansell Collection*

Part of the Hypostle Hall of the Temple of Amun-Re at Karnak,
built by Sethi I and Ramesses II   *Seif and Gaddis*

A relief on the south wall of the great temple at Abu Simbel
showing Ramesses II trampling on a prostrate enemy and
piercing a Libyan with a lance *Roger Wood*

The Battle against the Sea Peoples *Clarendon Press, Oxford*

Part of a fresco depicting the conquests of Ramesses II

The Mansell Collection

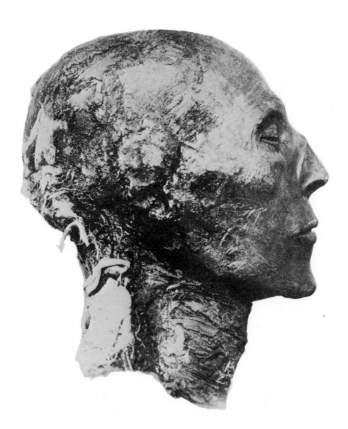

Profile of the mummy of Sethi I, now in the Cairo Museum

The Mansell Collection

A relief on the east wall of Abu Simbel showing Ramesses II
holding a group of Libyan and Negro prisoners by the hair

Roger Wood

10 The Last Great Victory

Throughout this book I have tried to show the durability and the resilience of Ancient Egyptian civilization. When Ramesses II fought the battle of Kadesh in 1285 BC, or thereabouts, this civilization had endured for at least 2,000 years, and it still had more than 1,000 years to run. During those twenty centuries there had been long periods of peace and prosperity interrupted periodically by civil war and even foreign invasion. But on each occasion, under the leadership of Warrior Pharaohs, Egypt had recovered and become even more powerful and rich. One has only to compare this with the record of other civilizations to realize that the Egyptians were either very fortunate or very plucky; perhaps both. Fortunate, in that for long periods they were protected from invasion by their natural defences, plucky, because when they were threatened they usually rose to the occasion and summoned sufficient resources of man-power and will-power to keep their way of life inviolate.

Compare the length of life of other civilizations which rose and fell in the Mediterranean and Near Eastern regions. The earliest, that of Sumer in the valley of the lower Euphrates, lasted at most for 1,100 years; Old Babylon, founded by Hammurabi, lasted 400 years, the Assyrian Empire for five centuries, the New Babylonian Empire for a mere seventy-six years. The Persian Empire lasted for less than 250 years, that of Greece (in her prime) about 400; the Minoans of Crete, down to the fall of Knossos in 1400 BC, can claim about 1,000 years; the Roman Empire of the west was in existence for half that period. Egypt lasted for over 3,000 years.

This could not have been a mere accident. We are so accustomed to the notion of perpetual change, which we call 'progress', that we may well be astonished at the conservatism of a people who could keep the same language, the same religion, the same system of government and the same way of life for more than *three times* the span of years which separates us from King Canute the Dane. Even more remarkable is that when these customs and this way of life were threatened by outsiders they fought hard and bravely to preserve it, to keep things as they were.

Some might be prepared to argue that this in itself does not prove that the Egyptian people did not want change; only that their rulers would not let them change; that they *had* to fight for their kings and priests whether they liked it or not. But this argument seems very doubtful. It is true that the Ancient Egyptian people did not choose their rulers but had to accept them. And it is true that a powerful tyrant or series of tyrants might force his will upon them for a time. But though there were weak kings and strong kings, and periods when central government appears to have collapsed, the Egyptians were always ready to respond if their land was threatened from any quarter, from the land of Kush, from the Libyans, or the 'vile Asiatics'. And if they had not liked their way of life why should they have been ready to fight for it, not for 100 or 200 years, but for 3,000? The answer surely must be that they thought so highly of the civilization which their ancestors had created that they thought it well worth fighting and dying for.

Before we go on to describe their last great victory against foreign invaders, we have to tackle that knotty question 'Which was the Pharaoh under whom the Children of Israel served? Which was the Pharaoh who, with his army, was destroyed when pursuing the Israelites?' Scholars have been trying to solve this problem for more than a hundred years, and are nowhere nearer a solution. Without trying to answer the question 'Is the Bible true?' we must first state that, whether one regards it as the inspired Word of God or not, it was written down by human hands.

Those hands wrote down the story many hundreds of years

after most of the events it describes occurred. Also the writers were not concerned so much with the history of the Jews and the peoples with whom they came in contact as they were with the developments of their religious beliefs.

So when we come to ask which Pharaoh it was whom Moses served we cannot be certain. Neither can we be certain even when Moses lived, except that it was obviously before the Jews settled in Palestine, when they were still wanderers. The general opinion seems to be that it was at some time between 1300 and 1200 BC, within the period of Ramesses II (1290–1224 BC) and his son and successor Mereneptah, the two greatest Pharaohs of this period. There is no record in any of the Egyptian chronicles of a disaster overtaking either of these Pharaohs, and the bodies of both have survived intact and mummified. (It could be argued, of course, that if one had been drowned in pursuit of the Israelites his body might have been recovered from the sea, but this seems a little doubtful, and neither body shows signs of having met a violent death.)

What adds still more to the mystery is that not only is there no reference in Egyptian chronicles to this event, but there is only one minute reference to Israel at all, and that occurs in an inscription set up by Mereneptah:

The princes are prostrate and cry 'Mercy'. Not one lifts his head among the Nine Bows [traditional enemies of Egypt], Tjehnuland is destroyed, Khatti at peace, Canaan plundered with every ill, Askhelon is taken and Gezer seized, Yeonam made as though it had never been. *Israel* is desolated and has no seed, Khor is become a widow for To-meri.[1]

There is also a reference, in another Pharaonic inscription, of a people called the 'Apiru' or 'Habiru'; it dates from the reign of Amenophis II (1436–1413 BC). For a long time some scholars have identified these people with the Hebrews of the Old Testament, but most Egyptian philologists (specialists in ancient languages) agree with Sir Alan Gardiner that it is simply a term meaning 'bandits' or 'outcasts' and therefore not necessarily connected with the Hebrews at all.

My own view is that there was an Exodus, that the ancestors of the Jews did sojourn in Egypt, and it is more than likely that some of them rose to high rank under the Pharaohs. But I think this probably occurred during the so-called Hyksos invasion, when many Semitic tribes, including the Hebrews, settled in the Delta. Some of their kings, e.g. Jacob-her, had Biblical names. But the story of the flight from Egypt, and the pursuit in which the Pharaoh's armies were drowned, probably dates from a later period and somehow got mixed up with the earlier chronicle. Who this Pharaoh was we have no means of knowing, and it is best to leave the subject to the shadowy realm between legend and fact to which so much ancient history belongs, not only in Egypt but in the early stories concerning Greece, Rome, and even Great Britain (e.g. the legends of King Arthur).

One fact must always be kept in mind. The Jews produced an immortal literature which has influenced us all profoundly through the Bible. But the Jewish tribes were, in military and political terms, never of much account in the days of Egypt's greatness. If they had been, then surely they would have been given an equally important place, in Egyptian records, with the Libyans, the Hittites, and the 'vile Kush'.

As for the parting of the Red Sea to allow the Israelites to cross, this depends on one's belief in the power of God to work miracles. If one does, then it could well have happened; indeed, anything could have happened. But it is a curious fact that a very similar story exists in Ancient Egyptian literature dating from the time of Snofru, father of the Pharaoh who built the Great Pyramid in 2700 BC. But this story is a charmingly frivolous one. While the King is boating on a great ornamental lake, accompanied by a number of young girl rowers, one of the girl's hair-ornaments falls into the water, and she refuses to row further until the King has recovered it. Snofru summons his Chief Magician, whose name was Zazamonkh, who waves his wand, parts the waters, and folds them back, leaving the bed of the lake dry. Then the lady recovers her ornament, the water is folded back, and the rowing continues.

None of the Pharaohs who followed Mereneptah were notable warriors, nor had they need to be, because the country was enjoying relative peace and security. The Nineteenth Dynasty ended in the year 1194, or thereabouts (the date is disputable), with the death of Queen Twosre after a reign of eight years. She was succeeded by Setnakhte, first king of the Twentieth Dynasty, who reigned for only two years, after which there followed nine Pharaohs all bearing the name Ramesses. Of these only one is of any importance, and that was Ramesses III, who reigned for thirty-one years, between 1182 and 1151 BC.

This period, the early and middle part of the twelfth millennium BC, was marked by great population movements all over eastern Europe and western Asia. New peoples were on the move, thrusting into Asia Minor and throwing out the Hittites, and into Greece, forcing the ruling power there, the famous Mycenaeans who had fought at Troy, to search for new countries in which to settle. Although the Ancient Egyptians knew the peoples of the Mediterranean (which they called 'The Great Green Sea') and had traded with them, they were too far off ever to be a menace – until now.

The Mycenaeans and the Minoans of Crete had been familiar with Egypt, and there are Egyptian tombs which show the envoys of these countries bringing the rare products of Mycenaean and Minoan manufacture – bronze swords and daggers, silver and gold goblets, fine pottery, to the Pharaoh. And in Greek literature, such as the *Odyssey* of Homer, we hear that Menelaus, after the sack of Troy, went to Egypt and brought back rich treasure to adorn his palace at Sparta, presumably taking Helen with him. In the *Odyssey* he shows off to Telemachus, the son of Odysseus, pointing to the Egyptian objects in his home, including a magnificent work-basket on castors, and a silver footstool, used by Helen.

It also seems highly probable that in the thirteenth century BC the Mycenaeans served as mercenaries in the Pharaoh's armies, and possibly even earlier than that; the gold with which the Mycenaean tombs were adorned must have come from Egypt, and some Greek scholars such as Professor Marinatos believe that the Mycenaeans got the idea of burying rich treasure with their dead from observing Egyptian funerary customs. But now, as the Egyptian chronicles report 'the Isles were in tumult'. Crete had fallen to the Mycenaeans some 300 years earlier, and now it was the turn of the Mycenaeans to be thrust out of their homeland. They were on the move, tough spearmen, mighty seamen, men whose ancestors had destroyed Troy. And the Trojans, too, were on the move, the Danaoi, whom the Egyptians called the 'Danu'. The Mycenaeans, whom they called the 'Achaiwasha', were probably Homer's 'Achaeans'. There were the 'Shardana', too, from Sardinia, tall men with feathered helmets and long swords who had fought as mercenaries in the Pharaoh's armies, the Shekel from Sicily, and, on the Palestinian coast, the redoubtable Philistines. All now became reluctant allies, since all had been dispossessed of their ancestral lands. Where were they to go in their search for new homes?

The answer was Egypt, and former Egyptian lands along the coast of Syria-Palestine.

Once again the Egyptians had to gird themselves for the fight, not only on land, where they were usually irresistible, but on sea, a more doubtful element in which many of the invaders were expert. Fortunately, in Ramesses III, they had a leader worthy of the emergency. Allowing for the inevitable boastfulness of the priestly inscriptions, the following account of the invasion and the events leading to it is one of the most thrilling documents to come out of Ancient Egypt. It should be read in conjunction with the magnificent picture of the famous 'Battle against the Sea Peoples' which Ramesses caused to be sculpted on the walls of his great temple at Medinet Habu in Thebes (Plate 29).

It begins: 'The foreign countries made a plot in their islands. Dislodged and scattered by battle were the lands all at one time, and no land could stand against their arms.' Foremost were the Khatti – the Hittites, Egypt's ancient enemies, who had been driven out of their homeland – but they had many allies from other lands, including Kode, Carchemish (a Hittite outpost in Upper Mesopotamia), Arwaza (in Asia Minor) and Alasiya. These were only a few of that formidable force which, sweeping down the coast of Syria-Palestine, set up a camp in the land of Amor (the Biblical Amorites) within easy distance of Egypt's frontiers. There were people called the Paleset – probably the Biblical Philistines, the Tjekker, the Sheklesh, the Danu (probably this refers to

Homer's famous 'Danaans' of the Trojan War) and the Weshesh. 'They laid their hands upon the lands to the entire circuit of the earth', writes the Egyptian chronicler, meaning, of course, the earth as known to the Egyptians.

Then follows a brief account of the military and naval preparations made by Ramesses III against this threat of invasion. 'I established my boundary in Djahi' (Palestine and Syria), prepared in front of them (the enemy) the local princes (Egypt's allies), garrison commanders and Maryannu. I prepared the river-mouth like a strong wall with warships, galleys, and light craft. They were completely equipped both fore and aft with brave fighters carrying their weapons, and infantry of all the pick of Egypt, being like roaring lions on the mountains; chariotry with able warriors and goodly officers whose hands were competent.'[1]

In the picture you will notice how the brilliant artist who designed it 3,000 years ago has succeeded in combining, in one illustration, the various stages of the battle. Remember that the original at Medinet Habu at Thebes is an enormous relief sculptured in stone and covering hundreds of square yards; and that what we have been able to show here is only part of the total picture. On the right Ramesses, treading on fallen enemies, is firing his arrows at the foe. Because he is both king and god he is naturally shown larger than anyone else. On the top left-hand corner is an enemy ship distinguished by its high prow and stern. Notice the characteristic horned helmets worn by the enemy.

Below it another enemy vessel, with a duck's prow, is in serious trouble. The foe, wearing feathered head-dresses, fall pierced by Egyptian arrows, and some tumble into the water. Spears fall thick among them and their yard-arm has fallen. Several enemies lie at the feet of an Egyptian officer who stands in front of Ramesses. To the left of this picture you will notice an Egyptian warship, distinguished by its long, rakish lines, low prow and stern, in which there is no confusion at all. The troops, wearing Egyptian wigs, are firing unperturbedly at the enemy while the rowers at their benches propel the ship resolutely forward. Notice the small figure of the helmsman with the larger figure of the archer standing on the poop above him. To the left other enemy vessels are in conflict, but getting the worst of it; many fall head-long into the sea.

And in the bottom row we see the victorious Egyptians march-ing in a proud line, driving the enemy prisoners before them. There can be no doubt about the outcome of this battle, the first 'combined operation' on record.

A net was prepared for them, says Ramesses, to ensnare them, those who entered into the river-mouths being confined and fallen within it, pinioned in their places, butchered and their corpses hacked up . . . As for those who reached my boundary, their seed is not. Their hearts and souls are finished unto all eternity. Those who came forward together upon the sea, the full flame was in front of them at the river-mouths, and a stockade of lances surrounded them on the shore.[2]

Egypt had been saved once again. The invaders, who had seemed invincible, who had marched down the coast of Syria and Palestine, accompanied by their baggage-wagons, their cattle, their women and children, and their fleet, were flung back in panic and disorder. Their proud ships had been sunk or scattered. Their warriors had been slain. Their plot, their Grand Design, had been brought to nothing. Wherever the survivors chose to settle it would not be in Egypt.

It was 2,000 years since Hor-Aha united the Two Lands. It was 400 years since Ahmose began to drive out the *hyksos*. It was more than three centuries since Tuthmosis III won the battle of Megiddo and 111 years after the Battle of Kadesh. As Ramesses III sailed triumphantly upriver to Thebes and heard the rising murmur of the crowds lining the banks; as the golden barges of the god Amun came out to meet him from the quays of Karnak, was he aware of the conquerors who had served Egypt centuries before he was born? Did he hear, above the clamour, the roar of Menkheperre's charioteers at Megiddo, or the high, clear scream of the trumpets before Kadesh?

Nothing comparable to this ever happened to Egypt again. Her civilization was to continue for another 1,000 years, but they would be years of slow, inevitable decline. Inevitable, because the changes taking place in the world outside Egypt could not be kept for ever beyond her borders. Slow, because her civilization was so old and deep-rooted that it took a very long time to die. Even during the period from 1100 BC down to 525 BC, before she became, for a short time, part of the Persian Empire, her authority in the Middle East was still enormous. It is mainly the petty Pharaohs of this period who are remembered with awe in the Old Testament. Yet compared with Tuthmosis III or Ramesses II, Shishak, who captured Jerusalem and took away the treasures of Solomon's temple (Twenty-second Dynasty, 945–730 BC), was a very minor Pharaoh indeed.

During those last 1,000 years she suffered the indignity of several conquests and foreign occupations, Babylonian, Assyrian, Persian, but when each of those empires had died Egypt was still there, and there was still a Pharaoh on the throne. The wandering Greeks established trading-stations in the country and renamed most of the cities the more easily to pronounce them. But the Greeks revered Egypt, and statesman such as Solon and travellers such as Herodotus left fascinating records of their visits in the seventh and fifth centuries BC. In those days the Egyptians were regarded by the Greeks as repositories of wisdom and knowledge, especially of science and medicine. But they had already, to a large extent, confused the various periods of their long history; or else the Greek writers misunderstood what they had been told. You will hear nothing of Tuthmosis or Sethi or Ramesses in the History of Herodotus, though a great deal about two monarchs called Rampsinitus and Sesostris, in which stories concerning Senusret and Ramesses II are curiously mingled. Most of what we know about the fighting Pharaohs of Egypt has come from the researches of Egyptologists over the past century; from Egyptian hieroglyphic records and from discoveries made in the tombs, especially those in the Valley of the Kings (the *Biban-el-Maluk* as the Arabs named it).

Over thirty of the greatest Egyptian Pharaohs were buried in that secret valley in which Ineni first hollowed out the tomb of Tuthmosis I, 'no one seeing, no one knowing'. All the great Tuthmosids were buried there; also Amenophis II of the great bow, Sethi I, Ramesses II and III and many others. Their predecessors among the warrior Pharaohs, such as Sekenre, who died wounds, probably when fighting the Hyksos, and Ahmose, who set in motion the process which was to drive those hated invaders out, were buried in tombs near the Valley. Each Pharaoh went to his 'House of Eternity' surrounded by a wealth of treasure. But all the ingenuity of the architects could not, in the end, protect these Pharaohs from the cunning and resourcefulness of the Ancient Egyptian tomb robbers, and by the Twenty-first Dynasty (945 BC) it is doubtful if more than a few of these Pharaohs' sepulchres had remained unrobbed.

In fact, we have actual records of trials held at the time of the Twentieth Dynasty (1184–1087 BC) in which certain malefactors were accused of making a regular practice of robbing the royal and noble tombs, and several admitted to it. Stricter measures were then enforced, and we know that when royal tombs were robbed – no doubt with the connivance of the guards – the furnishings were replaced, together with the bodies of the kings, if they survived. But eventually a time came when the priests responsible for guarding the Royal Valley found the task beyond them, and they hit on an ingenious and desperate plan. Instead of trying vainly to protect over thirty tombs, they thought, why not remove all the royal bodies and then rebury them in two sepulchres only, which would be easier to guard?

This was done. When, in Greek and Roman times, roughly between 330 BC and AD 300, visitors came to the Valley of the King's Tombs, they were shown only empty monuments, magnificent in their ruined splendour, their walls covered with sculptured reliefs and paintings, but containing no coffins and no gold-embellished furniture. Usually the sarcophagi, the stone outer coffins, survived, if they had not been broken by the ancient tomb robbers, but that was all. Of course, not all the Pharaoh's tombs were open. Some had become hidden by falls of rock and their very existence forgotten.

The Greeks came and went, and were in time also forgotten. The Romans occupied Egypt for a few hundred years and then they, too, became only a memory. The Arab invaders entered Egypt in the seventh century AD, but they were not very interested in Egyptian antiquities, and apart from the probings of a few curious

Caliphs the tombs were left alone. Twelve more centuries passed, and then European scholars became interested in Ancient Egypt and began exploring the Valley of the Kings and the adjacent cemeteries. They reopened many of the royal tombs and found them empty; they also noted, especially in the tomb of Sethi I, the smoke-blackened ceilings, the marks of earlier generations of visitors who had visited those tombs in Greek and Roman times.

The idea that the bodies of any of those Pharaohs could have survived, when their tombs had been robbed more than 3,000 years ago, was laughable. And then, one day, rumours reached Sir Gaston Maspero, the Director of the Antiquities Service in Egypt, that certain objects were appearing on the market which appeared to be royal, and that they appeared to be coming from Luxor (site of ancient Thebes). He started inquiries, and eventually the objects were traced to a certain family called Abderassul (Ab-de-ras*sool*), notorious tomb robbers and 'illicit diggers' in the Luxor region.

Repeated inquiries failed to reveal the secret, but as more and more objects appeared on the antiquities market bearing the signs of Pharaonic royalty it became clear that somewhere, somehow, someone had found a *cache* or storehouse of royal treasure. But where? Not in the Valley of the Kings, it was certain. Eventually, one member of the Abderassul family – persuaded by the local Turkish governor with the help of the *bastinado* (beating the soles of the feet) – gave away the secret. He and his brother had stumbled on a tomb, not in the Valley of the Kings, but on the eastern side of the mountain, containing over a score of mummified bodies, all with the royal serpent on their brows, and accompanied by small objects – a number of papyrus scrolls, jewellery, ornaments, etc. – which, being easily portable, the cunning Abderassul brothers had been feeding regularly on to the antiquities market. But they had not dared touch the mummies, since to do so would have invited too much attention from people who would have betrayed the Abderassul family.

When Maspero's deputy, Emile Brugsch, arrived and was lowered into the dark burial shaft, he found himself at the end of a long horizontal corridor stacked with mummies. This did not surprise him; there are millions of mummies in Egypt, mostly of ordinary people whose names mean nothing, But when Brugsch, who could read the hieroglyphs, raised his lamp and looked down on the inscriptions painted on the mummy wrappings he could hardly believe his eyes. In his own words:

> My astonishment was so overpowering that I scarcely knew whether I was awake or whether it was only a dream. Resting on a coffin, I mechanically cast my eyes over the lid and distinctly saw the name of King Sethi I, father of Ramesses II . . . a few steps further on, in a simple wooden coffin, lay Ramesses II . . . The further I advanced, the greater was the wealth displayed – here Amenopnis I, there Ahmose, the three Tuthmoses, Queen Ahmes Nefertari – all the mummies well-preserved, thirty-six coffins, all belonging to kings or queens or princesses.

The secret kept for 3,000 years was out at last.

The effect of this miraculous discovery on the Egyptological world was enormous. It seemed incredible that for some 3,000 years, while most of the known royal tombs had lain empty and plundered of their contents, their royal owners had slept secure and undisturbed in an obscure tomb less than a mile from the Royal Valley. There was evidence that before they reached this resting-place they had been moved several times, and the mummies rewrapped and relabelled by the priests. This was sufficient proof the the original tombs had been attacked on more than one occasion, but that each time the precious royal body had been saved and piously rewrapped. Ramessess III had been disturbed no less than three times.

Of course, nearly all the splendid funerary furniture had been taken, but the coffins were accompanied by a few small objects no doubt furnished from the Necropolis stores. In the heat of a sweltering July day, with the temperature in the hundreds, Brugsch and his assistants raised the royal bodies from their long hiding-place and transported them to the Museum steamer which was moored at Luxor. It is said that when at last the steamer began to move downriver to Cairo the local fellaheen (peasants) and their black-robed womenfolk moved along the bank, the men firing off guns as a last salute, and the women sending up the old wailing cry for the dead which had probably come down from the days of the Pharaohs. . . .

A few years later a French archaeologist, Monsieur Loret, began exploring in the Valley of the Kings. He came upon a tomb which had remained sealed for 3,000 years, that of Amenophis II, son of Tuthmosis III; this was the king who, as a young man, had shown such skill and strength with the oar in the 'falcon-boat' when he 'completed three *iteru* [four and a half miles] in rowing without rest from pulling the oar'. It was also Amenophis II of whom it was written that 'there was no one equal to him on the field of battle. He was one who knew horses, without his like in the numerous army, nor was there one in it who could draw his bow. . . .'

And there, lying beside the coffin, was the great bow itself, no doubt the very same one which the Pharaoh had carried into battle on many occasions. But Amenophis, though lying in his own tomb and in his original coffin, was not alone. All around him lay the bodies of other Pharaohs, some of whom had died before him, others after his death. For this tomb, because of its secrecy, was the second *cache* which the priests had chosen in which to hide other royal mummies. Among them was the great Mereneptah, son of Ramesses II, the Pharaoh whom, at the time, certain Biblical students had believed to be the 'wicked Pharaoh' of the Exodus who had been drowned in the Red Sea. There were altogether thirteen royal mummies in that tomb, including Tuthmosis IV and his son Amenophis III, the father of Akhenaten.

Today you can see these mummies in the Egyptian Museum in Cairo, each in a glass case with a purple cloth over it. The wrappings covering the faces have been removed, and it is an awesome experience to see, packed into one small chamber, the size of a largeish suburban drawing-room, all the great kings who have been the subject of this book.

Here is Sekenre, his skull gashed by hideous wounds, perhaps inflicted when he was fighting the Hyksos. There is Ahmose, one of his great successors who pursued the invaders into their home-land. Tuthmosis I is there, who 'raged like a panther' and 'cast the first lance' at the 'wretched Nubian Troglodyte'; so is Tuthmosis II. And next to him, looking strangely small, is the great Menkhe-perre, Tuthmosis III, himself, the 'scourge of the Asiatics', his round face with projecting upper teeth showing a distinct family resemblance to his father and grandfather.

Here is Ramesses II, who, at Kadesh 'arose like his father Mont and took the accoutrements of battle, and girt himself with his corselet', an old, old man with a fluff of white hair still bearing the marks of henna dye. He was probably nearly 90 when he died. And there is his father Sethi I, the most impressive of all Pharaonic faces, sculpturesque with its firm chin and strong, level mouth. It is, as one suspected, a face of great humanity. Almost equalling it in impressiveness is the mummy of Ramesses III; the hands are crossed over the breast, the broad handsome face has a slightly downturned mouth and a high brow. This, then, was the face of the man who saved Egypt from the 'Peoples of the Sea'. This was the body which stood poised, bow at the ready, in a war-chariot near the Delta; those dead eyes were the ones which saw the river-mouth alive with craft 'completely equipped fore and aft with brave fighters carrying weapons, and infantry of all the pick of Egypt, being like roaring lions on the mountains . . .'

To anyone with imagination the sight of these royal dead, especially after seeing their huge monuments, is almost unbearably moving. Originally each would have been surrounded by a king's ransom in golden treasure, and would have lain in a triple nest of coffins, the inner one, like that of Tutankhamun, being of solid gold. Yet here they are, little, parchment-skinned, shrunken corpses, as defenceless as when they came into the world. They, who once wore gorgeous raiment, must now be content with linen wrappings. Their world, which embraced huge countries, powerful armies and fleets, hordes of servants, and all the grandeur of high estate, has shrunk to this little room. They were men of action who must now for ever lie still.

---

1 Gardiner, A. H., *Egypt of the Pharaohs*, Clarendon Press, Oxford, 1961
2 Gardiner, A. H., op. cit.

Index

The Author

LEONARD COTTRELL began free lance writing while a writer-director for the British Broadcasting Company. After a few successful books, he resigned from the BBC to concentrate entirely on authorship. An amateur archaeologist from the age of 9, it was natural that his first book, when he was 29, was *The Lost Pharaohs.* The majority of his published works deal with early civilizations. Mr. Cottrell lives in Sussex, England, with his wife Diana.